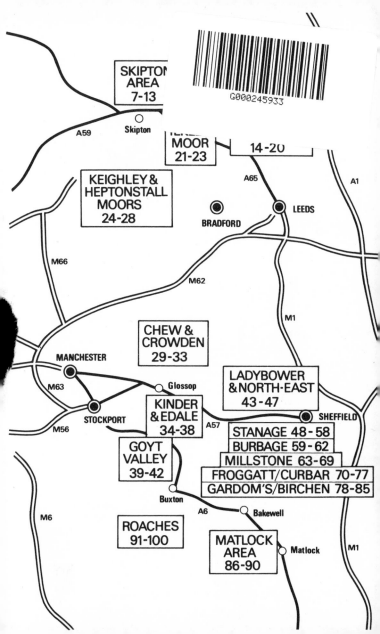

100 CLASSIC CLIMBS
– Yorkshire and the Peak District –

North-West Face, Almscliff

100 CLASSIC CLIMBS

YORKSHIRE AND THE PEAK DISTRICT
Gritstone

Steve Ashton

The Crowood Press

First published in 1990 by
The Crowood Press
Gipsy Lane
Swindown,
Wiltshire SN2 6DQ

British Library Cataloguing in Publication Data

Ashton, Steve, 1954–
    100 classic climbs on gritstone : Yorkshire and the Peak District
    1. Yorkshire. Gritstone regions. Rock climbing
    2. England. Peak District. Rock climbing
    I. Title
    796.5223094281

ISBN 1 85223 155 6

Picture credits
All black and white photographs, maps and topographical diagrams by
the author.

Typeset by Avonset, Midsomer Norton, Bath
Printed in Great Britain by Richard Clay Ltd, Bungay, Suffolk

Contents

Acknowledgements

Writing this book has been a solitary task. Likewise I have only myself to blame for the drawings and photographs. But the twenty years of climbing on grit, with or without this book in mind, have never been lonely, and for that I want to thank: Glenn Andrews, Tony Ashton, Dave Baines, Mike Combley, John Jackson, Jethro Jeffery, Crag Jones, Dave Knighton, Barry Owen, Dave Paxton, Alan Pinder, Dave Williams, Bern Woodhouse, and all those climbers who, perhaps seeing me soloing towards disaster, kindly offered me the end of their rope. Thanks also to Bill Wright of the BMC for advice on access matters.

Preface

Gritstone is the best rock in Britain, possibly the world. Some climbers dispute this, and they are to be pitied.

This book belongs to the *100 Classic Climbs* series, so I have had to cheat to bring you descriptions of more than 350 routes. What you have in your hands could more accurately have been titled '100 Classic Buttresses, Crags and Other More-or-less Definable Groups of Gritstone Climbs'. But that, you'll agree, has less of a ring to it.

Nevertheless, I had to leave out more than I could include. Much more. It broke my heart. Entire regions had to be scratched, whole crags omitted, and thousands of routes ignored, for the sake of producing a book that best serves the interests of visiting climbers.

Not that popularity was the sole criterion for selection, otherwise Stanage and the Roaches would have swallowed up half the book. Part of the appeal of gritstone is its great diversity, which is why such disparate crags as Simon's Seat and Dukes Quarry have been included.

I had to impose an upper limit on grades, or risk diluting the selection, and I make no apology for choosing HVS as the cut-off point, albeit stretched in a few special cases to E1. By the time you have outgrown these climbs, this book will already have served its purpose.

I felt I could describe only those routes I had climbed myself (though not necessarily as a leader). Inevitably this has resulted in a few notable omissions, most obviously that of The Sloth at the Roaches – an undisputed classic. For some reason I can't summon up the nerve to set off across that awesome roof. But the text mentions the line and suggests a grade, so don't hold back on my account.

The book is finished: routes checked, photographs taken, diagrams drawn. But I've not finished with the rock. When a climber grows weary of gritstone, he grows weary of life. Write that on your lavatory door.

S.A. 1990

Introduction

CLIMBING ON GRITSTONE

Gritstone occupies a special place in British rock climbing. Revered by some, despised by others, it is not a medium about which you can be ambivalent.

But how can these lichenous lumps of gritty brown rock, rarely more than 20m high, be so important? Partly because of their geographical distribution; a glance at the map at the beginning of the book shows that most of the outcrops are scattered along a backbone of high ground between major northern cities – Leeds, Manchester, Sheffield. For thousands of climbers, gritstone is the nearest rock they can lay their hands on. But it's more than that. There's an intensity about the climbing that brings it close to the idea of pure, unfettered movement. The rock is economical with its holds and clues, which makes for intriguing puzzles: regardless of route grade, there seems never to be more than just sufficient for the ascent.

Gritstone has other qualities. The rock, which is almost always sound, provides excellent friction; route lines are obvious and compelling; vegetation is minimal. But there's a price to pay: embedded quartz crystals mercilessly grind flesh from unhardened fingertips and knuckles. Unseasoned hands will not survive more than two successive climbing days.

For all its tough exterior, gritstone has suffered many kinds of assault over the years. Scars from the worst attacks – hold chipping – will not heal in centuries. A few days of rain washes away the evidence of the most recent form of abuse – chalk. But not from beneath overhangs, and not during the weeks of drought. Arguments to restrict its use to climbs above a certain grade are worthless. At this late stage of the debate the only sensible plea is the one for restraint – by everyone. It feels good to climb a route with a minimum of chalk, and a chalk-free ascent comes closest to the ideal.

REGIONAL INTRODUCTIONS

The crags have been grouped into sixteen regions, each introduced by a page of general description. In most cases a map accompanies the text. This shows crag location, road approaches, parking places, and so on. Each introduction also includes a brief note on access.

ROUTE INFORMATION

Route descriptions are gathered under a section heading, of which there are 100. Most sections include a collection of routes from a prominent face or buttress, others cover an entire crag, while a few deal with just a single route. There is no hard-and-fast rule on groupings so don't equate overall quantity with individual inferiority; often the allocations were made according to the convenience of illustration.

Each section begins with some general information:

Summary: A brief resume of what is on offer, perhaps indicating the range of grades or the ambience of the crag.

Crag Conditions: An indication of altitude, aspect, drying time, setting, and popularity. This will help you choose an appropriate venue whatever the season or prevailing weather.

Approach: Information to get you from the main road to a convenient parking place, and up to the crag by the recognised approach, along with an indication of walking time. Parking places and crag locations are also identified by grid references (eg: GR:674 235). If a crag is subject to an access restriction then a note to consult the regional introduction appears here.

ROUTE DESCRIPTIONS

A preliminary paragraph outlines the main features, nature of the rock, average route length, and perhaps a reference to a convenient descent.

Routes are identified by section and diagram numbers. For example, route 74.3 will be shown on the Section 74 crag diagram by the number 3. All this becomes fairly obvious as you flick through the guide.

Unlike previous books in this series, route descriptions are quite specific. One reason for this is that on gritstone an error of just one metre can put you in an entirely different bracket of difficulty, or even on an entirely different route. Another reason is that gritstone routes are often chosen according to the nature of climbing on offer: one person's dream jamming crack is another's worst nightmare.

ROUTE DIAGRAMS

The topo diagrams used in other books of this series would serve no useful purpose on grit so route lines are shown on conventional crag drawings. These are based on photographs taken from normal viewing points, so the main features should be readily identifiable without having to view the crag through a telescope from the opposite side of the valley (there *are* exceptions, necessitated by dense woodland or a steep slope below the crag). Some drawings have been distorted to offset the effects of foreshortening.

Almost always the route diagram appears below or opposite the description. If not then this is made clear. In a few cases, for practical reasons, one of the route lines may not appear at all. An arrow on the drawing indicates its whereabouts and the deficiency is made good in the text.

GRADING

This is the difficult bit. The overall (or adjectival) grades have been abbreviated as follows:

M	Moderate	**S+**	Hard Severe
D	Difficult	**VS−**	Mild Very Severe
D+	Hard Difficult	**VS**	Very Severe
VD	Very Difficult	**VS+**	Very Severe (Hard)
VD+	Hard Very Difficult	**HVS**	Hard Very Severe
S	Severe	**E1**	Mild Extremely Severe

Nothing too controversial here, except perhaps the three-tier *VS* grade, which has been brought in to ease congestion. *E1* is the top grade in this selection, though others up to *E8* have been mentioned.

Technical (or numerical) grades have been appended to routes graded *VS−* and upwards. They are: 4b, 4c, 5a, 5b, 5c.

Interpreting Grades: A route grade is not sacrosanct. It is merely a symbol that warns you of how vigorously the route is likely to fight back if you try to climb up it. Nothing more, nothing less.

Most of the route grades in this book are undisputed. Others have been eased up or down a notch to achieve some sort of consistency across the regions. The biggest problems arise when attempting to compare the difficulties of climbing incomparable rock features, such as a vertical jamming crack and an unprotected bald slab. You've got to assume that the reader has served a broad-based gritstone apprenticeship and is as capable of jamming up a *VS* crack as frictioning up a *VS* slab.

Any subtlety in the system comes from the precise combination of overall and technical grades. Consider the grades of these two neighbouring routes at Froggatt: Tody's Wall (VS+,5b), Three Pebble Slab (E1,5a). Which is the harder route? According to the technical grades, the crux of Tody's Wall (a weird mantelshelf just above a ledge and runner) is more difficult than anything on Three Pebble Slab (a sustained and unprotected series of breath-holding balance and friction moves), and yet no-one who has seen or climbed the routes will be in any doubt as to which is the more difficult proposition from the leader's point of view.

National Equivalents: Gritstone technique is so peculiar, so personal, that attempts to compare grades with those used elsewhere in Britain would be misleading. For myself I find that my top leading standard on grit is at least a full grade down on what I can expect to climb in, say, North Wales. Others (admittedly a minority) find the situation reversed. My advice is to start modestly and gradually build up a feel for what you can realistically attempt.

International Equivalents: Attempts to equate gritstone and international grades are even more futile. However, to give a broad indication, the following grades are roughly similar:

British	UIAA	USA
VD	III+	
S	IV+	
VS	V+	5.7
HVS	VI	5.9
E1	VII–	5.10a/b

Star Ratings: You might have expected all routes to warrant three stars for quality, but then some classics are better than others, which is acknowledged in the difference between ✦✦✦ and ✦✦. The ✦ routes have been thrown in for good measure, or because they are individually ordinary but collectively classic (the routes at Windgather and Castle Naze come to mind). Don't take these ratings too seriously: if a route has been selected then, without exception, it is worth doing.

ACCESS

Not all crags lie within national park boundaries, and of those that do, many are on private land with no automatic right of access. This is not the place to argue the rights and wrongs of land ownership, so advice in the regional introductions merely reflects the current response to specific access problems. These responses may change from time to time, as relations with tenants and owners improve or sour, or as land moves in and out of public hands. The British Mountaineering Council (BMC) can advise on the changing access situation (Crawford House, Precinct Centre, Booth Street East, Manchester M13 9RZ. Tel:061-273 5835). Bulletins also appear in *High* magazine, their official journal.

Because a crag appears in this book it doesn't mean you have a God-given right to climb on it (or, if you prefer, that everyone else agrees with your God-given right to climb on it). In the most sensitive areas it is often only through the continuing efforts of local climbers and the BMC that access is maintained.

Most access problems could be averted if climbers tried harder to minimise their impact on the land, and on those who live and work there. Inconsiderate parking, straying from approach paths, damaging fences and walls, leaving closed gates open, letting dogs off the lead, leaving litter, and generally making a noise, are all guaranteed to infuriate not only other climbers, but also the people who can and will reverse an access agreement.

METRIC UNITS

Given that in Britain we are perpetually hung between metric and imperial measurements, I have been forced to botch together some sort of compromise:

Route lengths are given in metres (m). If you don't like them pretend they are yards: and if you don't like yards, multiply by three and call them feet. Altitudes and walking distances are also given in metres, ostensibly to conform with OS maps. Road distances are given in both kilometres (km) and miles. The first on principle, the second to conform with milometer readings.

MORE INFORMATION

Maps: In theory you should be able to reach any crag aided only by approach instructions and the regional map. All the crags described in Sections 30-100 appear on the 1″ OS Tourist Map to the Peak District, so that may be worth buying. At 1:25,000 scale, the two Outdoor Leisure series maps to the Peak District (White Peak and Dark Peak) cover almost the same area in greater detail, though of course at greater cost. OS maps for the Yorkshire regions are less convenient. Most of the crags are near roads anyway, so perhaps the only map worth considering is the Yorkshire Dales (Southern Area) in the 1:25,000 Outdoor Leisure series, which includes the more remote crags collected under the Skipton Area heading.

Comprehensive Guidebooks: Between them the Yorkshire Mountaineering Club and the BMC publish a full set of comprehensive guidebooks to the main gritstone areas. To match the coverage of this book you would need to buy seven. The total cost would be ten times or more what you paid for this one, but then the *depth* of coverage would be far greater. Once you have got to know a region through this guide it makes sense to buy the appropriate comprehensive guide. That way you can compile a full library gradually, yet without in the meantime confining the scope of your climbing to its growth.

Travel and Accommodation: The gritstone area is so diverse that I have made no attempt to list the availability of public transport, official campsites, bed & breakfast accommodation, and other local services. If you need this information on arrival then the Yellow Pages are your best source. Unofficial camping is widely discouraged, so this is rarely a practical alternative to using established sites (dossing in vans and bivouacing in caves is another matter).

EQUIPMENT

Everyone who climbs regularly on grit will have their own preferences for gear so I'll direct these remarks to those coming to gritstone for the first time:

Rope: Most routes are best climbed using a single rope. It's faster and more convenient. On the few occasions when a double rope is necessary, it is usually possible to double the single rope.

Hardware: No need to carry a full rack of nuts. By all means bring along a wide selection in the sack, but you should be able to select out half a dozen just by looking up at the route. In general there's little call for micro nuts and small wires, whereas camming devices are more than usually useful. They're ideal for plunging hurriedly into jamming cracks or protecting otherwise hopelessly flared horizontal creases, though something a little more passive is better for stuffing behind flakes. And bring along that cow-bell hex you've never used – could be just the thing for that evil off-width.

Helmets: Not many of these in evidence at Stanage on a Sunday, but that's not to say they have no use. A helmet won't make much difference in a head-first plummet to the ground, but it could if you swung into a corner, or fell backwards among boulders. Stonefall is a real possibility at a couple of the crags with bands of shattered rock near the top, Millstone Edge being the prime example. Otherwise the greatest risk is from kids tossing rocks over the edge for a lark.

Approach Wear: Trainers or other lightweight footwear are adequate for approaches during dry weather. At other times, lightweight boots might be preferable for walking up to the more remote crags. Some of the moorland crags are situated at altitudes of 500m or more, often in extremely exposed locations, so take what food and clothing you would for a mountain day in Wales or the Lakes.

A FINAL CAUTIONARY NOTE

I have yet to find a completely error-free guidebook. Logic tells me that this one, despite all my efforts, will be no different. I can only promise that I have done my best. I have also tried to purge ambiguities from the text, but I'm aware that personal knowledge of a route may have blinded me to the inadequacies of its description. If you discover any mistakes, or misjudgements on grades or route quality, or have any other suggestions to make that might improve the guide, then please write to me, care of The Crowood Press.

Brimham Rocks

Brimham Rocks are situated near the northern limit of Yorkshire gritstone country. A famous geological curiosity, they have been brought under the protection of the National Trust. The weird rock formations – the result of wind and water erosion but once thought to be the work of Druids – attract so many visitors that climbers are easily outnumbered.

From a climbing point of view there are two areas of particular interest: the numerous pinnacles scattered about the grounds of Brimham House, and the edge which bounds the area to west and north. Woodland paths weave through the pinnacles, adding to the fairytale atmosphere; it is difficult (but wise) to take the climbing seriously. Climbing on the edge is more conventional in appearance and execution. It is also more secluded on busy weekend afternoons.

Sightseers preceded climbers by many years, Brimham Rocks having become part of the tourist circuit as early as the eighteenth century. In 1895, we are told, three thousand people, a brass band and a choir of a hundred gathered here for a Wesleyan rally. Perhaps some of the youngsters scrambled up the pinnacles and got themselves stuck, much as they do today. Not before the 1950s did climbers come in strength and with serious intent to Brimham. Hatter's Groove and Allan's Crack are products of this period, though some of the easier classics – Lover's Leap Chimney among them – had been climbed long before that.

It would be unfair to single out for special mention any of the pinnacle routes because so much of their charm depends on the company and the mood of the day. Of those on the edge, Lover's Leap Chimney and the adjacent Birch Tree Wall easily qualify as the outstanding classics of the rocks.

The rock is eminently sound. It has a reputation for brutal roughness, though only on overhanging jam cracks, where the quartz pebbles bite deepest, does this become painfully evident.

Approach: From the A59 Skipton to Harrogate road. Turn north on the B6451 to Summerbridge then follow signs to Brimham Rocks for about 3km/2 miles. There are large car parks (fee during peak periods) at the south end of the rocks. GR:208 647.

Access: This is National Trust property and so there are no access restrictions. Dogs should be kept on a lead or, better still, left at home.

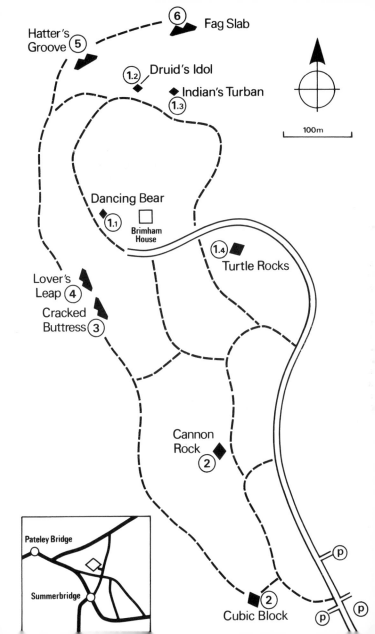

Hatter's Groove ⑤

⑥ Fag Slab

Druid's Idol ①.₂

Indian's Turban ◆

①.₃

Dancing Bear

①.₁ ◻ Brimham House

①.₄ ◼ Turtle Rocks

Lover's Leap ④

Cracked Buttress ③

100m

Cannon Rock ②

Pateley Bridge

Summerbridge

Cubic Block ②

1: BRIMHAM – THE PINNACLES

Summary: A small number of solo 'fun' routes and short conventional climbs selected from the dozens of pinnacles scattered throughout Brimham's enchanted garden.

Crag Conditions: Lack of drainage and vegetation ensures that all routes dry quickly. Some routes face south, so there is scope too during sunny winter days. Climbing here during summer weekends is to risk a great deal of public attention (and possibly embarrassment).

Approach: (Refer to the regional introduction for general location.) The selected routes ascend pinnacles situated in the vicinity of Brimham House: refer to the map accompanying the regional introduction for specific locations.

Exploration and discovery are the great delights of climbing on Brimham's pinnacles, so only a few of the easier and more prominent ones are described. In most cases a rope is a hindrance to enjoyment, and provides little security for the leader. Route lengths range from 5-8m. Sooner or later, every visitor to Brimham gets stranded on top of a pinnacle. In some cases the way down is, alas, the reverse of the way up.

1.1 Dancing Bear (D+) ❊
A small distinctive pinnacle set uncomfortably close to Brimham House and subject to scrutiny from its visitors. Very much a solo route. Shelving steps on the west side lead to a final pull through a slot. Descend the same way, rather awkwardly.

1.2 Druid's Idol (VD) ❊
A small, improbably poised, and infuriatingly rounded pinnacle. A solo problem. If all else fails, try traversing anti-clockwise from the south corner and finishing through a slot above a big ledge on the north side. Descend by the same route until low enough to jump.

1.3 Indian's Turban West (VD+) ❊
The west face of the larger of twin pinnacles. Feels serious, despite its small size, thanks to an insecure mantel just below the top. Descend on the east side via the intimidating crack between the two pinnacles (natural thread if required).

1.4 Turtle Rocks Chimney (VD) ❊
Start up the big chimney followed by a pull onto a ledge on the north side of the Turtle Rock itself to bring the top within reach. Descend by abseil or by reversing the ascent to the ledge and leaping the chimney to the far side, from where there are several easy descents.

DRUID'S IDOL

INDIAN'S TURBAN

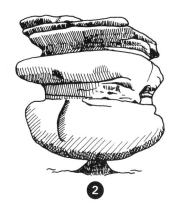

DANCING BEAR

TURTLE ROCKS

2: BRIMHAM – CANNON ROCK AND CUBIC BLOCK

Summary: A selection of low and middle-grade routes on two of Brimham's larger pinnacles. The vertical prow of Cannon Rock contrasts with the slabby face of Cubic Block.

Approach: Refer to the regional introduction and its accompanying map for general and precise location. Both pinnacles lie just a few minutes from the car parks.

Crag Conditions: As for Section 1.

Not all Brimham pinnacles are small and friendly, and by the time you arrive at the 10m Cannon Rock, rising prow-like from its leafy surrounds, it will not be too soon to uncoil the rope. Cannon Route exploits a slanting weakness on the west side, while on the east side Maloja uses a grooved weakness to the left of the thin cracks of Frensis Direct (E1,5b). Descend by ledges on the north side (or reverse Cannon Route for more interest).

The slabby 10m east face of Cubic Block provides a number of low-grade balance climbs and also the more testing arete of Cubic Corner. The Block also has its dark side; the overhanging west face climbed at E3 and E4. The merely vertical north face is climbed by Rough Wall (VS,5a). Descend to the south over blocks.

2.1 Cannon Route (D) ✳
Start on a boulder beneath a large ceiling on the west side and traverse left, finishing awkwardly through a break in the overhang.

2.2 Maloja (VS–,4b) ✳ ✳
A fine miniature climb with a memorable crux. Pull onto a ledge on the east side and climb a cracked groove. Boldly pinch a fluting to gain good flat holds for the short traverse left. Finish easily past the Cannon Hole.

2.3 Old Corner (VD) ✳
The shortest and easiest route on the slab. Climb the left edge via a wide crack at mid height.

2.4 Heather Wall (VD+) ✳
There's a hard start to gain a mantelshelf at quarter height, and another awkward move to gain the crack above.

2.5 Great Slab (VD+) ✳
Starts with good intentions up the middle of the slab then loses nerve at a niche and traverses right for a finish near the arete on good but spaced holds.

2.6 Cubic Corner (S+) ✳ ✳
The right arete. Tension mounts in direct proportion to the ground fall consequences.

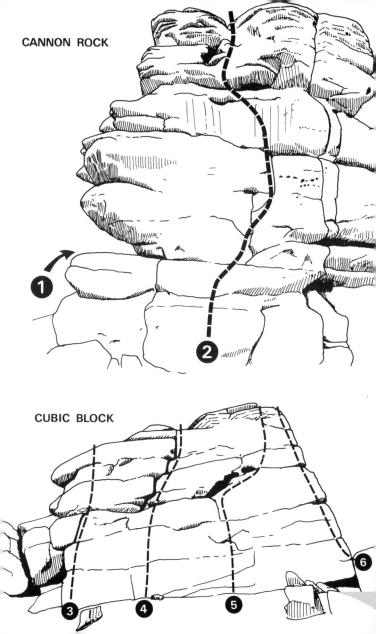

CANNON ROCK

CUBIC BLOCK

3: BRIMHAM – CRACKED BUTTRESS

Summary: A pair of characteristic jamming cracks marred by insecure exits. A simple corner crack and a clean chimney provide easier alternatives.

Crag   Conditions: South-west facing, free of vegetation, and quick to dry. Druid's Chimney lies within a shady recess and so will hold dampness longer.

Approach: Refer to the regional introduction for general location, and its accompanying map for specific directions. Can be reached from Cubic Block (Section 2) by walking north along an overgrown path, though most easily gained by walking south from Brimham House to Cleft Buttress (identified by its radiating passages) then turning north-west to arrive at the buttress in less than 100m. 10 minutes from the car park.

Brimham is renowned for its brutal cracks. The centre pair of this set of four look innocent enough – until you get within pawing distance of the top where the comfortable hand cracks widen to arm-width flares. Nothing on Stanage will prepare you for the grovelling true finish of Central Crack. The right-hand line on the face – Cracked Corner – is simple and uncomplicated, whereas the left-hand line of Parallel Cracks (VS,4c or harder) maintains the theme of hard exits. A better route is that of Druid's Chimney tucked out of sight further left. Route lengths range from 10-12m.

3.1 Cracked Corner (D+) ✳
Thankfully this pleasant corner crack has nothing in common with its senior neighbours.

3.2 Right-Hand Crack (VS,4c) ✳ ✳
The most enjoyable of the cracks. The first section of the crack succumbs to layaways, the smooth centre section to jamming, and the wide finish to other means.

3.3 Central Crack (VS+,5a) ✳
A short groove and clean jam crack of perfect width lead pleasurably to a ledge below the appallingly insecure exit fissure. Those doing this for fun rather than through a misguided sense of duty will escape right to finish up the Right-Hand Crack at 4c.

3.4 Druid's Chimney (S) ✳ ✳
A surprisingly good chimney climb up the back of the recess which bounds the left side of the buttress. Try to work things so you're facing left at the crucial middle section, making best use of a flake on the left wall. Above, some honest back-and-footing leads to a ledge from where the boulder overhangs can be bridged out.

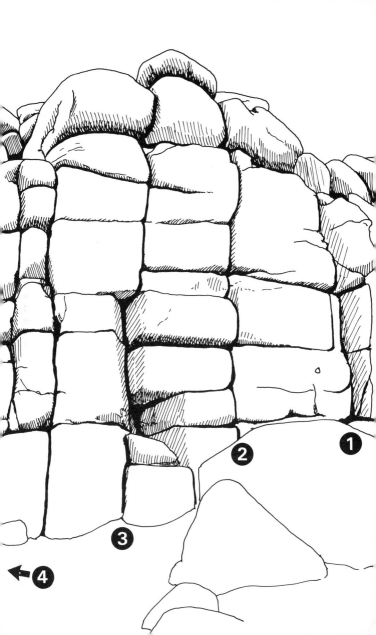

4: BRIMHAM – LOVER'S LEAP

Summary: A large, cleft buttress harbouring a contrasting pair of Brimham classics: an atmospheric chimney and a poorly-protected face climb.

Crag Conditions: Faces west and takes little drainage. The interior of the chimney is protected from showers but will take longer to dry after heavy rain than will the more open Birch Tree Wall. Sloping holds and poor protection on Birch Tree Wall imply that it is worth waiting for absolutely dry conditions.

Approach: Refer to the regional introduction for general location, and its accompanying map for specific directions. The simplest approach is via Cracked Buttress (Section 3). 10 minutes from the car park.

Appropriately the two finest and longest (15m) routes at Brimham are found side by side; the first enclosed and mostly secure, the second open and mostly unprotected. Sandwiched between is the neo-classic Left Wall (E5,6a).

4.1 President's Progress (VD) ✳
Worth doing to wind down from (or wind up to) an ascent of Lover's Leap Chimney. Start to the right of the main recess, at a short corner below a severely overhanging chimney, and layback with effort to a large ledge. Creep through a hole to a platform (which could have been reached much more easily from directly below) then bridge the square-cut recess above.

4.2 Lover's Leap Chimney (VD+) ✳✳✳
One of the top-ten grit chimneys. A huge chock guards direct entry so start up a strenuous flake crack in the left wall and, protected, step right to gain the first platform at a junction of secret passages. Boulders choke the main throat of the chimney above, though they at least provide some thread protection for the energetic bridging required to surmount them. Ignore the through-route exit and finish with a final flourish outside of the top chockstone, emerging at an iron guard-rail fitted, one assumes, to give spurned lovers time for second thoughts.

4.3 Birch Tree Wall (VS, 4c) ✳✳✳
Elegant but serious climbing. Beyond a hard start, a slim groove ends with a tricky move up to a small ledge on the right. Now traverse delicately left and move up to gain a leftward-slanting ramp which, though initially delicate, progressively eases. A protectable but inferior 4b variant start traverses in from the left to meet the main line after its own delicate traverse.

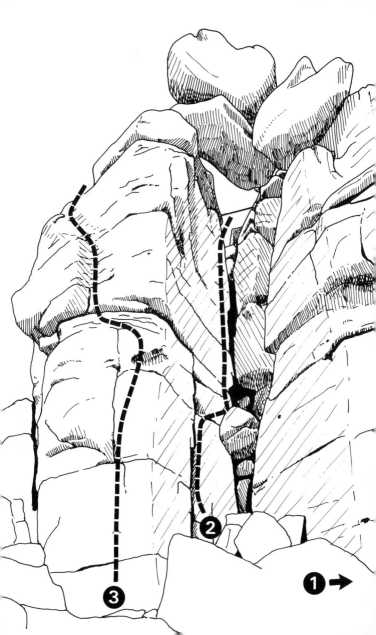

5: BRIMHAM – HATTER'S GROOVE AREA

Summary: A gloomy buttress containing an intimidating V-groove of some renown.

Crag Conditions: North-west facing and slow to dry.

Approach: Refer to the regional introduction for general location, and its accompanying map for specific directions. Can be reached from Lover's Leap (Section 4) or more directly via Brimham House and the Druid's Idol. 15 minutes from the car park.

Few sightseers stray to this secluded part of the edge so there is some compensation for its sunless aspect. Hatter's Groove is one of Brimham's 'big feel' routes, seemingly much longer than its actual 12m.

5.1 Hatter's Groove (HVS,5a) ✳ ✳
Sustained bridging and back-and-footing leads over a bulge to a final overhang and, thankfully protected by a good thread, a desperate exit left.

5.2 Slippery Crack (S+) ✳
A semi-layback start on good footholds ends with an awkward pull into a wider crack, which is laybacked for real towards a rounded ledge and an exit assisted by a Thank God pocket.

5.3 Last Crack (S+) ✳
All attempts to avoid laybacking this cracked corner will be thwarted.

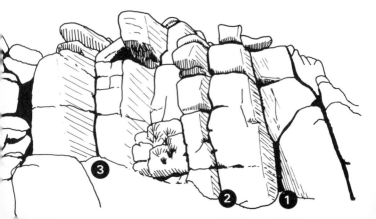

6: BRIMHAM – FAG SLAB AREA

Summary: A secluded, slabby buttress climbed by delicate minor routes and a major *VS*.

Crag Conditions: North-west facing and slow to dry (though not as tardy as Hatter's Groove).

Approach: As for Section 5 then continue north-east for about 150m. 15 minutes from the car park.

The 8m Fag Slab shares the seclusion of the Hatter's Groove area without suffering its oppressive gloominess. Allan's Crack presents a bigger (13m) and more varied challenge.

6.1 Fag End (S+) ☀
Delicate, unprotected climbing on chiselled holds. Shameful yet delightful.

6.2 Fag Slab (S) ☀
Sustained yet reasonable climbing up a shallow, unprotected groove.

6.3 Fag Slab Variant (VS–,4b) ☀
This superior variant approaches the Fag Slab groove via layaways and friction holds under the slanting overlap.

6.4 Allan's Crack (VS,4c) ☀ ☀
A major Brimham route marred only by an unexceptional finish. Protectable. Layback the initial leaning corner then use pocket holds on the slab to circumvent the overhang and regain the good layback crack above. Good holds lead out right beneath the top overhang for a finish near the arete.

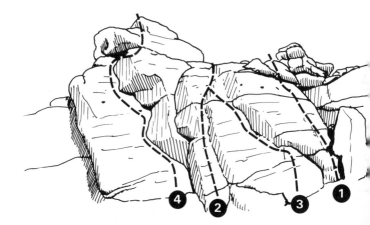

Allan's Crack (6.4), Brimham

Maloja (2.2), Brimham

Skipton Area

Set far from the industrial heartland, isolated outcrops on the moors north of Skipton are preserved in rural tranquillity. Nowhere is this more apparent than at Simon's Seat, the most remote of Yorkshire's gritstone outcrops. The crag lies at the summit of a grouse moor; a bleak climbing ground in bad weather, but a refuge from heat and crowds in high summer. Its finest climbs could stand alongside the best at Almscliff.

Closer to Skipton, the crags on the fringe of Embsay Moor are less dramatic in outlook but offer climbs of equal quality. Most intriguing is Eastby, which not only faces south – a rare treat on Yorkshire grit – but has been pushed back by some almighty hand to a comfortable slab angle and then had its holds removed. What might have been a beginners' playground has become a test of nerve for *VS* leaders as they teeter up protectionless friction slabs.

Crookrise is the most extensive edge in this group. It looks out from its moorland setting over a plantation, but the trees do not encroach and, when clouds permit, it basks in afternoon sunshine. No single style of climbing predominates; there are as many slab and face climbs as cracks and overhangs. Of the many good routes to be found among the jumble of buttresses, none could be described as individually great (with the possible exception of The Sole). It is the crag as a whole, not one route in particular, which leaves the most lasting impression.

Rylstone, cursed (or blessed) by a northerly aspect and long approach, remains comparatively neglected. Those who persist will be rewarded with solitude and two splendid slab routes.

Access: All four crags in the group are set on grouse moors and are subject to closure for up to thirty days during the shooting season (12 August through to December), though not simultaneously and not on Sundays. Fire risk may also prompt closure. Closure notices are posted in advance at access points to the moors. Dogs are banned at any time.

Special permission is required to climb at Eastby. The present arrangement is to phone the Bolton Abbey estate office (0756-71227), and to maintain the goodwill of the tenant farmer Mr Danvers of Dale Head Farm, Eastby (near the pub).

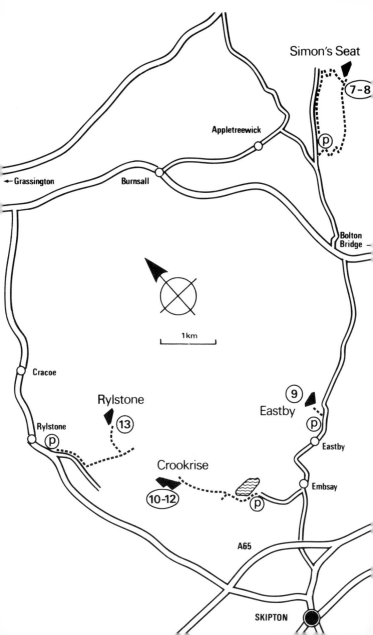

7: SIMON'S SEAT – LOW NOSE

Summary: Disjointed routes finding some good move sequences on a blocky buttress. A remote moorland setting provides traditional atmosphere.

Crag Conditions: Faces north-west in an exposed position at an altitude of 475m and is therefore frequently cold and slippery (a small nearby buttress – not described – faces south-west). Worth waiting for warm, dry weather. The rock is a lichenous coarse grit; the aretes and thin cracks are clean and solid, whereas the chimneys and gullies tend to be scruffy. Though the crag stands just below Simon's Seat summit, a popular local walk, it remains hidden from view and retains its remote feel. Seldom are there more than a couple of climbing parties at the crag.

Approach: Refer to access notes in the regional introduction. From Bolton Bridge on the A59 Skipton to Harrogate road, take the B6160 towards Grassington for 5km/3 miles, passing Bolton Abbey, then turn right for Appletreewick. Fork right after 2.5km/1.5 miles onto Howgill Lane and park after 400m, where a track leads off to the right from a gate (GR:063 592).

Follow the winding track uphill (ignore left forks in the forest) to open country. Continue on the main track as it veers left above the top wall and follow it north-east over the moor to the summit of Simon's Seat (GR:079 598). Note that the first rocks to come into view are those of the small south-west face; the main crag lies hidden below the north-west side of the actual summit. 45 minutes.

For a good alternative return to the valley, descend north and follow a zig-zag path down to Dalehead Farm (GR:075 605), from where the Howgill Lane leads left back to the parking area.

The main climbing area at Simon's Seat consists of a shady back wall curving forward into two wings – High Nose on the left and Low Nose on the right. Continuous lines on Low Nose are mostly dirty chimneys so the three selected routes, all about 20m long, weave among the cleaner intervening buttresses looking for excitement.

7.1 Simple Simon (S) ✴✴
There's a hint of mountaineering in this introductory route, though the name hardly conveys what trials lie ahead. The initial slabby wall leading to a ledge is easy enough, whereas the pod-shaped recess on the right gives a few anxious moments of (protected) thrutching and bridging to better holds in the crack. A seemingly innocuous but baffling overlap split by an off-width crack is best overcome facing left by a layback move. A leaning fissure above a rocking boulder is the final obstacle, though it can be side-stepped on the right.

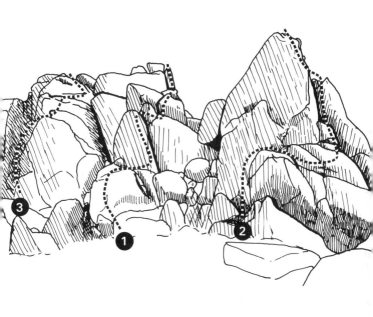

7.2 Low Nose Traverse (VS,4c) ✳

A devious and difficult approach to the cracked front of Low Nose itself. A high runner protects a teetering friction traverse right, which is partially aided by rounded handholds and a hidden undercut. Once gained, the wide crack soon gives up so swing left above it for a fine arete finish on good holds.

7.3 Winter Finish to Griffith's Chimney (VD) ✳

A surprisingly interesting climb, and not too difficult. Start up the dirty rift of Griffith's Chimney then, at a steepening, walk right across a dirty ledge which apparently leads nowhere. Peer round the arete to discover a horizontal crack for hands and runners – one or other of which may become stuck as you make the crucial move up. Semi hand-traverse a right-slanting crack on good jams to finish up an easing crack slanting back left.

Arete Direct (8.2), Simon's Seat

8: SIMON'S SEAT – HIGH NOSE

Summary: A pair of technically trying routes – a bold layback and a balancy arete – taking the best lines on a remote moorland outcrop.

Crag Conditions: As for Section 7.

Grades assume crisply dry rock. The Arete, free of drainage, dries quickest but is exposed to strong winds.

Approach: As for Section 7.

The leaning cracked groove at the left side of the back wall, and the clean edge of High Nose itself, both about 18m high, easily justify the long approach walk.

8.1 Turret Crack (HVS,5a) ✳ ✳
Elegant from afar, this slightly overhanging groove looks distinctly ugly from close up. Confident laybacking leads past a partial rest at a shallow pock-hole to a good landing on the half-height ledge. Step left to gain the easier upper crack.

8.2 Arete Direct (VS,4c) ✳ ✳ ✳
Potentially the most enjoyable route on the crag. Unlike most gritstone aretes, this one can be adequately protected. Semi hand-traverse left between overlap and undercut base to gain the arete at a big spike. Climb the arete close to its crest on layaways, with a harder move at half height.

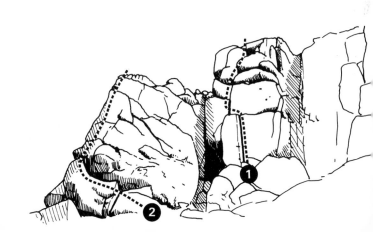

9: EASTBY CRAG – PILLAR AND NOSE

Summary: A large, slabby buttress climbed by poorly-protected
friction routes.

Crag Conditions: South facing
at 300m. Pleasant when fine,
diabolical when wet.

Approach: Refer to access notes
in the regional introduction. From
Skipton take the minor road north-
east through Embsay. Park on the left
midway between Eastby village and
an S bend (GR:022 546). Approach
via gates marked with access
notices. 10 minutes.

Eastby is unique in Yorkshire in that the whole crag lies back at a slabby angle.
However, this is more than offset by the paucity of holds and protection. Typical
route length is 18m.

9.1 Nose Climb (VD+) ✳✳
Traverse parallel break lines to a ledge on the nose. Layback the nose to a
friction slab and finish by a crack on the right.

9.2 Eastby Buttress (VD) ✳✳
The best of the easier routes. Step left from beneath the big roof and move up to
better holds. The groove continuation is heathery so finish up cracks in the left wall.

9.3 Pillar Rib (VS−,4b) ✳
A variant on the previous route, climbing the crack and rib to its left.

9.4 Whaup Edge (VS,4b)✳✳✳
Bold climbing up an undercut arete. Enter from the right and climb the arete
on friction and layaways to the mid-height break (dubious runners). Continue
in the same breath-holding manner until the arete becomes usefully sharp.

9.5 The Padder (E1,5a) ✳✳
The name and grade says it all. Climb the middle of the slab on pebbles (crux)
to the mid-height break. Slightly easier padding leads to a slot exit.

9.6 Swastika (VS+,5a) ✳✳✳
A wandering line culminating in an ascent of Whaup Edge. Layback to an
easement in the left-bounding groove. Get established above the undercut
and traverse the Pillar to a belay in the heather groove. Traverse right to finish
up Whaup Edge.

9.7 Pillar Front (E1,5a) ✳✳✳
A tremendous route up the Pillar, flawed only by opportunities for escape.
Climb the overhang just left of the arete and step up to a rare good runner.
Climb the 'ramp' diagonally leftwards on friction and pebbles (crux) to a
foothold on the arete. Pull over the overhang on pockets and balance up to the
right. Trend left to finish.

THE PILLAR

THE NOSE

10: CROOKRISE – BLACK GULLY AREA

Summary: A variety of crack and face routes in the *S* to *HVS* grades on a sunny and secluded crag, the best of them being a well-known climb of formidable difficulty.

Crag Conditions: In general the edge faces south-west, so despite an altitude of 375m it can be pleasantly warm. The trees of Crookrise Wood do not encroach significantly at the crag base, allowing the generally vegetation-free buttresses of typical rough grit to dry quickly.

Approach: Refer to access notes in the regional introduction. From Skipton town (not the A65/A59 by-pass) take the minor road north-east to Embsay. Follow the minor Pasture Road west from the Elm Tree Inn (the elm a mere twig of its former self) to the end of the surfaced section. Park on the verge (GR:001 543). Walk up the track past the sailing club and reservoir to the moor gate. Cross the stile and follow the path rising left, alongside a wall, to the fell top (ignore the crag on the left halfway up – Woodside Buttress). Cross a ladder stile and descend through boulders to arrive at a large slab – End Slab – at the right-hand side of the main crag. The Black Gully area lies 50m further left (GR:988 558). 30 minutes.

End Slab can be climbed by some diverting if contrived routes: Route One (VD+) gains the sloping shelf near the right edge then traverses the break left to finish up a wide crack, while Edge Variation (S) climbs the right edge via a pocket.

The Black Gully recess contains several notable climbs, from the 8m extended boulder problem of West Wall Climb to the rambling 12m routes of Craven Crack and the nearby Chimney Variation. Nevertheless, it is the sustained 10m of The Sole up the left edge of the protruding right-hand buttress which attracts all the attention. The quickest descent is by Black Gully itself, the rift between the two buttresses.

10.1 The Sole (HVS,5b) ✳ ✳ ✳
A desperate start eases through a strenuous middle section to a merely difficult finish. Protection is available for those with the stamina to place it. A slim groove indents the left edge of the buttress front and is climbed by an out-of-balance layback (crux) to a brief respite at the overhang. A couple of moves up a finger crack on the left side of the arete (5a) gain good holds and protection at the horizontal cracks. Traverse the cracks steeply left and move up to finish by a wide crack.

10.2 West Wall Climb (VS,4b) ✳
Climb the left side of a blunt angle in the short wall left of The Sole. The holds are good but spaced, and there is no worthwhile protection.

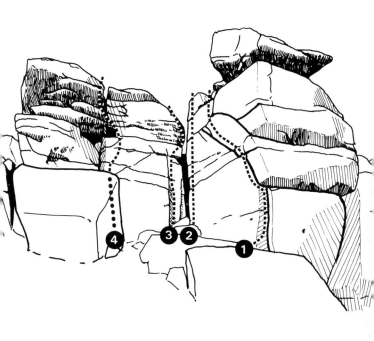

10.3 Craven Crack (S) ✳

Takes the crack in the wall left of Black Gully, with a few gymnastic moves to start. Protection and holds are good. Move right at a ledge to finish over bulging rock (a crafty back-kick on the far side of Black Gully restores lost balance).

10.4 Griffith's Chimney Variation (VS,5a) ✳

The lower part of Griffith's Chimney itself looks gruesome and is liable to be wet. The variation uses a 5a problem start, easing to poorly protected 4b moves, up the arete to its right. From a ledge, an exit up the final part of the chimney is not difficult (or try climbing the overhang above the middle of the wall on the right).

11: CROOKRISE – ARSENIC SLAB AREA

Summary: Contrasting routes in the middle grades: a slab, a jamming crack, and a chimney.

Approach: As for Section 10. Continue leftwards below the crag for another 50m.

Crag Conditions: As for Section 10.

The 12m Arsenic Slab is a larger version of End Slab, and its routes equally contrived. Open Chimney and the traditional Long Climb (15m) ascend breaks in the wall to its left.

11.1 Arsenic Slab (VD+) ✳
Climb the undercut start of Diagonal Crack (VD) then traverse delicately left. A brave (i.e. unprotected) pull on the flakey right edge of the prominent block gains an easing slab finish.

11.2 Long Climb (S+) ✳ ✳
Exposed at the overhang, though well protected. Pull strenuously over the undercut start from a ledge at 2m and climb more easily to the overhang. Surmount the overhang on good jams then stomach traverse left to find the wall finish.

11.3 Open Chimney (VD) ✳
An antidote to Arsenic Slab. Exit awkwardly left at the first chock and pass the second more easily on the right. Avoid a plodding finish by finishing up the right arete.

12: CROOKRISE – SLINGSBY'S CHIMNEY AREA

Summary: A classic *V.Diff* chimney and some wandering *VS* face climbs.

Approach: As for Section 10. Continue leftwards below the crag for another 150m.

Crag Conditions: As for Section 10.

12.1 Flake Wall (VS–,4b) ❄❄
The slabby right wall of the buttress. Climb a slanting crack to the right of the boulder arch, finishing with a mantel. Step up and left from a nut slot (crux) to finish near the left edge on improving holds.

12.2 Slingsby's Chimney (VD) ❄❄
Struggle up the outside of the first section then bridge and back-and-foot the yawning upper chimney.

12.3 Chimney Buttress (S+) ❄
Avoid the best bit of the chimney by traversing a ledge leftwards from the chockstones to an unprotected finish up rounded rock.

12.4 Crease (VS,4c) ❄❄
Traverse a line of pockets (possible Friend/Hex protection) and make a committing move high or low around the blunt arete to better holds. Trend left then finish straight up (the obvious direct start is 6a).

12.5 Rushlight (VD+) ❄
A pleasant filler up the slabby wall left of the break.

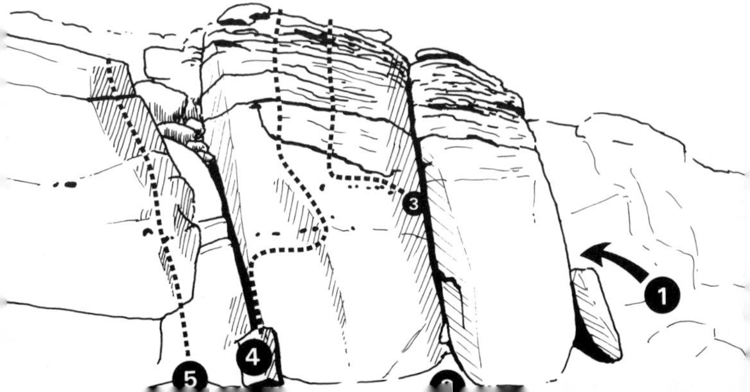

Slingsby's Chimney (12.2), Crookrise

Crease (12.4), Crookrise

13: RYLSTONE – MAIN CRAG

Summary: Two fine, comparatively long climbs in the lower grades on the slabby rock of a remote moorland outcrop. Dental Slab is a classic of the region.

Crag Conditions: This moorland outcrop faces north-west at an altitude of 425m and is therefore often cold and greasy. It is best reserved for a warm, dry day.

Approach: Refer to access notes in the regional introduction. From Skipton, take the B6265 north towards Grassington. Park on the roadside at GR:971 583, 250m south of Rylstone village (room for 2 or 3 cars). Resist attempting a direct approach to the crag and instead, from 50m south of the parking area, turn left on a bridleway. From a gateway (marked 'access gate') follow a track uphill past a group of conifers towards the crest of the moor to the right of the crag (identified by the prominent Rylstone Cross). Break off left at the crest and go up between the top of the crag and a wall (ladder stile on transverse wall) to the top of the main crag 300m beyond the cross. GR:986 578. 45 minutes.

Despite the long approach walk, Rylstone warrants a visit from the *Severe* leader anxious to collect all of Yorkshire's prize routes at this grade. Dental Slab is not to be missed. Though the neighbouring President's Slab does not quite have this stature, it does make a worthwhile second route. At 18m both are longer than average, though the old guidebook's recommendation that President's Slab provides 'good training for the would-be alpinist if done with a full pack' rather stretches the point (you get all the training you need from the walk-up). The two slabs, 30m apart, are the most obvious features on the main part of the crag.

13.1 President's Slab (D+) ❊ ❊
"Slab" adequately describes the angle but not the technique: this series of semi-mantelshelves will sap energy unless completed efficiently. The route can be protected with large nuts. A good direct start (VD) ascends from the pointed foot of the slab on sloping holds (and an odd foot-in-pocket move) to the horizontal break where the ordinary start comes in from the left. A sequence of semi-mantelshelves up horizontal breaks leads to a ledge and, if required, thread belay. The second section trends rightwards to a crack then diagonally left, with interest, to finish on good holds.

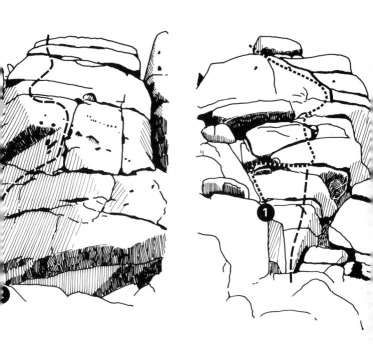

13.2 Dental Slab (S) ✷ ✷ ✷

As good as any *Severe* slab climb on grit. Follows a satisfying, protectable line up the left side of the big slab. Start on the left below the undercut base of the slab then, after a step up, traverse right (with protection) and pull up at the nose using a big pocket. At the next break, a move or two higher, traverse left on parallel horizontals and then climb a slight ramp – not obvious from below – up to the right. After moving left again, carefully choose the best place to mantel onto a sloping break so as to reach good holds at the top.

Almscliff/Caley Area

Situated close to the Leeds/Bradford conurbation, it is no surprise that Almscliff and Caley are among the most popular of Yorkshire's gritstone crags.

Almscliff is perched on top of a hill within view of Lower Wharfedale. This elevated position attracts many sightseers, when it isn't attracting bad weather, though spectators rarely outnumber climbers. The crag was once notoriously undergraded, and reputedly there are no good routes at a genuine low standard. This is untrue. Low Man provides some useful introductions – Fluted Columns the best of them – while there are several good and fairly graded *Severes* on the South and South-West Faces. That said, the climbing here does require a positive approach, and few are unmoved by the intimidating sight of the North-West Face – the major section on the crag. Here is the finest concentration of middle and upper grade climbs on Yorkshire grit, many of which are too difficult for this selection. Nevertheless, all the best lines are included: Great Western, that magnificent route climbed in the 1940s by Arthur Dolphin; Frankland's Green Crack, of pre-1920s vintage; the spectacular Parson's Chimney; and Overhanging Groove, considered by many to be the most enjoyable route on the face.

Caley, though pleasantly situated on a thinly-wooded and boulder-studded slope, never fully escapes the traffic noise of the main road below. The crag, or more correctly the cluster of outcrops and boulders, poses a problem for this book because most of the big routes on the Main Crag are either too hard or too unattractive for inclusion. Besides, most people come here not for the routes at all but to 'play' on the boulders. In an attempt to resolve this, the selection comprises only the easier routes on the Main Crag plus sufficient boulder problems to serve as an introduction. Come here any fine evening or weekend and you will see dozens of other good problems demonstrated first-hand.

Access: There are no access restrictions at Caley, and none at Almscliff provided the crag is approached as described, and that the boulder in the walled field below Low Man remains out-of-bounds.

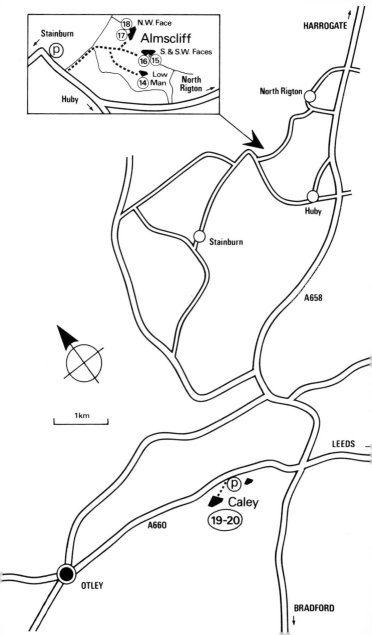

14: ALMSCLIFF – LOW MAN

Summary: Useful introductory routes in the lower grades on a minor buttress of Yorkshire's most famous gritstone crag.

Crag Conditions: Though set at a lowly 175m, Almscliff sits astride an exposed hilltop among treeless pastureland – a comfortless place to climb in blustery weather. On calm days, Low Man and the South and South-West Faces provide pleasantly warm conditions. Though greasy when wet, the rock takes little drainage and soon dries out. The crag is extremely popular during summer evenings and at weekends.

Approach: Refer to access notes in the regional introduction. From the A658 Bradford to Harrogate road, turn off for North Rigton or Huby and in either case take the minor road to Stainburn. After about 1.5km/1 mile – the crag will now be obvious up on the right skyline – there is a tight left-hand bend with parking for several cars (avoid blocking gates). GR:265 491. A public footpath leads from a stile near the bend to the crag in a few minutes. Refer to the inset map accompanying the regional introduction for the arrangement of buttresses.

Low Man is the poor relation of the Almscliff buttresses, lacking both the ferocity of the North-West Face and the variety of the South and South-West Faces. Nevertheless, this is the best place to introduce yourself to the crag, which has a reputation for rebuffing first-time visitors. Fluted Columns makes a pleasant opening, while Square Chimney is more typical of the obstacles that await on High Man. Route lengths range from 10-13m.

14.1 Square Chimney/Whisky Crack (S+) ❋
Climbs a shallow and deceptively awkward converging chimney then finishes up a more predictable jamming crack. Gain a shelf awkwardly then chimney up, facing right, to reach a tiny ledge on the right. Resist abandoning everything for the mantel and keep chimneying until you can get your foot on the ledge. An awkward step up gains the midway ledge and, if required, a block belay on the left (which could have been gained from the left with a lot less anguish by V Chimney (VD)). Whisky Crack can be started direct but is more usually entered from the left via the block. Once entered, it gives widish hand jamming to a reachy leftward exit (belays well back plus a fluting above the ledge).

14.2 Fluted Columns (VD+) ❋ ❋
The best route on Low Man; open and momentarily exciting at the crux. Start just to the right of an unpleasant-looking chimney and gain shelves by a couple of unprotected step-ups. Above the second shelf, which overlooks the chimney/crack, the eponymous flutings protect a balancy move up (finger-pocket above the bulge) and exposed step left. Finish on good holds near the crack.

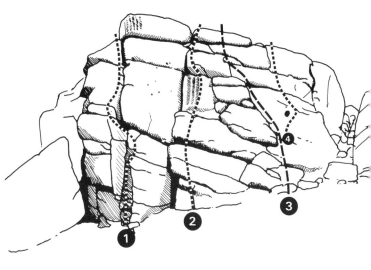

14.3 Low Man Easy Way (M) ✳

A mostly simple right to left diagonal following the big flake, a prominent feature of the slabby right-hand side of the face. Where the flake gives out, the angle eases to give a straightforward finish just to the right of Fluted Columns.

14.4 Stewpot (VD) ✳

An undistinguished variation on the previous route, incorporating a couple of good moves. Quit the Easy Way at the first shelf and head for the large pock-hole on chipped footholds. Avoid the hole on its right with a delicate step, then move back left to finish up a wide crack.

15: ALMSCLIFF – SOUTH FACE

Summary: A traditional chimney thrutch with several, intriguing variant starts.

Crag Conditions: As for Section 14.

Approach: As for Section 14.

Variation starts to South Chimney possess such independence of character that this is really three routes in one. Taken direct the chimney gives 10m of climbing. Descend as for Section 16.

15.1 South Chimney (D+) ✳ ✳
Clean and classic. Face left to thrutch the narrow lower section and overcome a chockstone to enter a recess. Climb the upper chimney facing left.

15.2 South Face Start (S+) ✳
Begin up a polished, right-trending gangway right of the chimney then move left and mantel (crux). Move up left to gain the chimney. (Birdlime Traverse (HVS,5a) traverses the overhung fault rightwards from above the mantel.)

15.3 Slab or Wall Start (VS,5b) ✳
Gain the ledge part way up South Chimney via the slabby easement on the left (shallow pockets and friction) or via the intervening wall.

15.4 Layback Start (S+) ✳ ✳
Layback and jam the crack well to the left of the chimney then traverse the overhung ramp rightwards into the chimney.

SOUTH–WEST FACE
(16)

SOUTH FACE
(15)

16: ALMSCLIFF – SOUTH WEST FACE

Summary: A compact face climbed by a popular *Severe* crack and a couple of short, stubborn climbs with off-width entries.

Crag Conditions: As for Section 14.

Approach: As for Section 14.

Though slightly lower than the South Face – the direct routes barely attain 10m – the South-West Face is more extensive and offers a series of climbs begun on time-consuming cracks of unhelpful widths. The more predictable Bird's Nest Crack provides a good introduction to gritstone cracks. Descend easily left or right, or by scrambling down Three Chockstones Chimney in the middle of the face.

16.1 Stomach Traverse (VS,5a) ✳

Immediately left of the fenced wall is an undercut off-width. Either pull over the bulge to the right of the crack and climb the face – strenuous with long reaches – or fist jam direct into the crack and exit with a long reach. Climb a simple crack above, step right onto sloping shelves, then finish easily trending left.

16.2 Central Crack (S+) ✳

Another baffling entry, this time into a holdless runnel (try a right-facing layback). The upper crack widens horribly to get round an overhang, so step right from an overhung corner to climb the face, pulling back into the crack above the overhang. An easier option is to finish up Stomach Traverse.

16.3 Crack and Wall Traverse (VD+) ✳

Devious but finds the easiest way up the face. Layback the corner near the left end of the wall then sidle rightwards across the ledge to Central Crack. Continue the traverse to gain the upper, easier part of Stomach Traverse.

16.4 Bird's Nest Crack (S) ✳ ✳

A well-worn but excellent route. Sustained but protectable and with no nasty surprises. Climb the crack on good jams then trend right to the projecting hold. Use this to reach more good holds and finish with a secure jamming move. For the variation start (VS−,4c), layback the thin crack to the right, move precariously onto a good hold on the left, then continue up and left to join the original. (Demon Wall (HVS,5a) traverses left out of Three Chockstones Chimney at one-third height to climb a bulging wall.)

Great Western (17.1), Almscliff

17: ALMSCLIFF – NORTH-WEST FACE (Right Side)

Summary: An imposing face of bulging rock climbed by a fine chimney and two of the great Yorkshire 'VS' classics. (Refer to Section 18 for crag diagram.)

Crag Conditions: As for Section 18.

Approach: As for Section 14.

The best and most famous Almscliff routes are concentrated on the intimidating North-West Face, where the lines are at once both compelling and repulsive. Great Western climbs the overhung corner on the right then traverses left above a bulging wall taken by Western Front (E3,5c) and, further left, Wall of Horrors (E3,6a). Long Chimney takes the big slit to the left, and Frankland's the stepped corner left of the detached Pulpit pinnacle. (Refer to Section 18 for descents.) The routes are over 15m in length, and feel much longer.

17.1 Great Western (HVS,5a) * * *
Three stars are not enough. The crux arrives at the moment of maximum exposure and commitment. Layback and jam the undercut corner to a partial rest where a slanting crack arrives from the left (high runners). Hand-traverse left (more protection in a horizontal slot) until the wall bulges beneath. The object now is a gargoyle above left, but the crack leading to it is unhelpfully wide so try laying away using a pocket on the right and, higher, a good hold on a block. All very dramatic and strenuous. The gargoyle provides a crouching rest for the jamming exit up a short, bulging crack.

17.2 Long Chimney (D+) * * *
Full of foreboding, runners and bird droppings. Face left and use a crack in the left wall for feet and runners to secure a sustained bout of chimneying to the chockstone (belay if required). Escape via a through-route or finish outside the top chockstone.

17.3 Frankland's Green Crack (VS,4c) * * *
The green crack is deeply recessed and dark with overhangs, giving few hints of the superb climbing to come. Protection and rests arrive between each difficult sequence. The big overhang is almost, but not quite, by-passed using wall holds on the right. At the moment of truth, bravely layback (or cowardly jam) the wide crack to get stood up on the crease level with the overhang. Climb the upper crack to a resting niche below the top overhang then surmount it with some wide bridging.

18: ALMSCLIFF – NORTH-WEST FACE (Left Side)

Summary: A clean wall, fissured and indented, containing a famous chimney and a superb groove climb.

Crag Conditions: Refer to Section 14 for general conditions. The North-West Face is especially exposed to wind and, denied the sun until late in the day, often feels cold and cheerless. Obviously it takes a little longer to dry than the other faces, although the green appearance of the rock is deceptive.

Approach: As for Section 14.

The left side of the North-West Face is less imposing than the right. Though barely less high (15-17m), the overhangs are less massive and the lines more continuous. Parson's Chimney is the dominant feature – Overhanging Groove being, in effect, a direct finish to its left-hand start – while Central Climb and Z Climb find ways up the cracked face to its left (the much sought-after North-West Girdle (E1,5b) begins up Z Climb, traverses to Long Chimney at half height, then finishes at three-quarters height by reversing the Great Western traverse). Descend by scrambling over boulders to reach a gully on the north-east side, well to the left of the climbs, or by West Chimney (M) to the right of the face.

18.1 Parson's Chimney (S+) ✳ ✳ ✳
A great climb which, after an open and insecure start, delves into the depths of the chimney before making a sudden, breath-taking bid for the top. Start to the left of the lower continuation to the chimney (the difficult direct start) and layback a groove on polished footholds, suppressing survival instincts for the sake of urgency. At its end (runner for the second!) traverse into the chimney for a belay. For the upper section, start at the back of the chimney and work upwards and outwards facing right, then change direction for an exhilarating exit on good holds.

18.2 Overhanging Groove (VS+,4c) ✳ ✳ ✳
A near-perfect gritstone route, potentially the most enjoyable on the North-West Face, with the crux where it should be – near the top. Short climbers must substitute dynamism for lack of reach. From a rest and runners above the Parson's Chimney layback start, ascend the shallow and slightly overhanging continuation groove in an orgy of bridging, long reaches and jug pulling.

18.3 Central Climb (VS–,4b) ✳ ✳
Ascends a system of face cracks on the wall to the left of Parson's Chimney. Although there are good holds and protection possibilities after every move, the wall is set at such an angle that it is difficult to rest and place runners. With plenty of stamina and a considered approach it will feel straightforward,

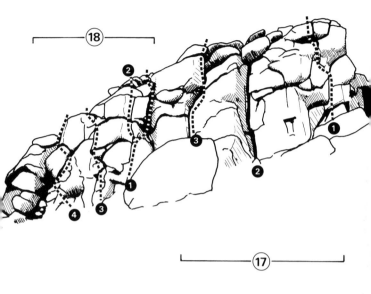

otherwise not. The line itself is obvious: climb up to the niche and then trend left to finish.

18.4 Z Climb (VS,4c) ✳

A useful addition to the face, incorporating three interesting problems, but with a disappointing finish. Gain a sloping ledge on the left side of the face by an energetic and unprotected 4c finger traverse from the right. After placing protection, climb a bulging and initially over-wide right-slanting crack until it narrows to a more comfortable hand width, then hand-traverse left to a ledge. If the absence of runners here makes a bold finish up the slabby wall unjustifiably serious, consider finishing up the blunt nose a little to the left.

Overhanging Groove (18.2), Almscliff

19: CALEY – BOULDERS

Summary: Suggestions for problems and miniature routes on the
numerous excellent boulders
situated around Caley Crag.

free-standing boulders and so take
longer to dry. Extremely popular,
especially on spring evenings, but
the atmosphere is friendly.

Crag Conditions: Set at 150m on
a north-facing hillside. Some faces
catch the sun, depending on the
season and time of day. Most
boulders take no drainage. However,
a few are small outcrops rather than

Approach: As for Section 20 for
the Sugar Loaf. For Roadside Buttress, pass through the gate and find
a path leading leftwards across the
hillside for 100m or so to the crag.

Some problems are actually miniature routes, and failure at the crux might
lead to a twisted ankle or worse. A rope is not out of place on some of the
longer ones. The boulders are found in two distinct groups: the Sugar Loaf
area near the Main Crag, and Roadside Buttress on the hillside to the east.
Only a few introductory problems are described; the rest await your
rediscovery.

19.1 The Sugar Loaf (D/HVS) ✳ ✳
Lies adjacent to the track when approaching the Main Crag. The slabby south
face gives several D-VD slab routes (easiest descent down the left edge). The
west wall can be climbed by Route One (VS,5a), starting up the middle then
following a right-slanting line, or straight up the middle on fingery layaways by
Route Two (VS,5a). The east wall, high and bulging, is climbed by Angel's Wall
(HVS,5a).
   The clean wall opposite the Sugar Loaf has twice been chiselled into
submission. Both are just high enough and hard enough (5a/b) to give a buzz
at the finish.

19.2 Roadside Buttress (S/HVS) ✳ ✳
The main group consists of three north-facing walls set back in a sequence of
three to the left. The right-hand, front wall can be climbed by the obvious
Morris Crack (S), precariously laybacked up its sharp left edge, or by the
steepening Morris Slab (S) to its left. After a dynamic start to get established
above the undercut, Rabbit's Paw Wall (HVS,5b) climbs the middle wall by
trending left on pockets and flake side-pulls to a reachy finish. The
disappearing crack on the wall round the left arete is Unfinished Crack (VS,4c),
while Little Cenotaph (VS,5a) struggles up the corner to its left.

20: CALEY – MAIN CRAG

Summary: A varied selection of middle-grade routes on a north-facing crag, from back-and-foot chimneys to delicate slabs.

Approach: Via the A660 Leeds to Otley road. Park on the verge near Caley Gate (GR:230 445) at the start of a bridleway which slants up the hillside, past the Sugar Loaf boulder, to the crag. 10 minutes.

Crag Conditions: The main crag generally faces north and is slow to dry in winter, though individual faces may catch the sun in the morning or evening during summer.

Despite some fine routes, the main crag at Caley is less popular than the boulders scattered beneath. For this reason the described routes have been selected from the lower grades, these being generally under-represented on the boulders.

The dominant feature of the crag is a deep bay in its left side. This is bounded on the left by a smooth wall and the terrifying arete of High Noon (E4,6a), and on the right by a leaning wall cut by two repulsive-looking fissures – Block Chimney (VS,4c) and Compulsion Crack (VS+,5a). The crack at the back of the bay is Lad's Corner (VS,4c). The described routes ascend the friendlier area of slabby walls and perched blocks to the right. Route lengths range from 10-15m. Descend between the main group of climbs and the buttress containing Zig-Zag.

20.1 Pedestal Wall (S) ✻ ✻
Slow to start, but worth doing for the exposed finish on a slabby wall. Climb up the slabby face of slipped blocks to the right of the bay to a ledge and thread belay at the foot of the pedestal. A short chimney on its left side gives an awkward moment on small holds until good pockets can be used to move up and across to the left edge for a friction finish.

20.2 Rib and Slab (VS–,4b) ✻
Exquisite if aimless climbing on a delicate rib and slabby wall. There is no protection, though a controlled slither from the top slab ought to be halted by the midway ledge. To the right of Pedestal Wall a huge block lies against the wall. Climb the rib at its right edge in a series of layaways – the hardest moves being at the start and at half height. From the halfway ledge, move a little to the left and climb the middle of the upper slabby wall.

20.3 Square Chimney (VD) ✻
Surprisingly good, with more exposure than you would expect. Back-and-foot the chimney formed between the huge block and the right wall of the corner (runner at half height), stepping left onto the rib to avoid the small capstone.

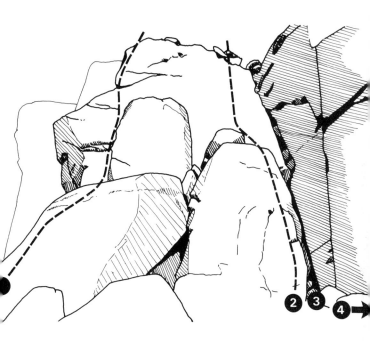

Climb the top corner facing right to discover huge holds on the overhanging right edge of the chimney (natural chock runner halfway). Take care to find the best holds to complete the gritty, exposed finish.

20.4 Zig-Zag (S) ✤
Not outstanding, but a useful addition to the main routes. Protectable. It takes the vertical front face of the buttress 20m right of Square Chimney. Starting a few metres right of the left arete, climb a dirty corner to a grassy ledge. Now climb a strenuous, though not difficult, crack and move left to a small ledge and optional stance (an exposed variant finish – The Scoop (VS,4c) – trends left from here). Hand-traverse the wide crack rightwards on jams and either continue by this method to exit at a ledge, or, when possible, step up to reach good handholds.

Ilkley Moor

Perched on the moor edge high above Ilkley town, the Cow and Calf Rocks symbolise the dual escapist function of Yorkshire gritstone outcrops; many people come exploring here, and committed climbers are in a minority. Thousands of adventurous children must have discovered the terrible delight of rock climbing by clambering up the hewn steps of the Calf. The Cow, a huge lump of mostly holdless grit, has also suffered at the hand of the chippers, though here they have been rather more discreet. 'A' Climb finds a natural line for itself, traversing out onto the main face for an exposed finish. Good climbing: great atmosphere. It is even more impressive when combined with the exposed variant finish of Ferdinand.

The next group of climbs is hidden from view in a nearby quarried bay. Within its echoing calm, climbers creep along polished ledges and struggle up polished cracks as they have since the 1930s. The face is small by quarry standards, so can hardly be expected to produce truly excellent climbs, yet the intricate Walewska qualifies, and S Crack is almost as good.

The third group of crags adds another facet to the character of Ilkley Moor. Rocky Valley is just what is sounds like: a crease in the moor overlooked by scattered buttresses. Some of the routes here are popular, though in general Rocky Valley is spared the constant attention bestowed on the Cow and Calf and the Quarry. Number Six Buttress, largest of the crags, offers that long-standing favourite Spreadeagle, while Number Two provides the best of the easier routes with Flake Climb, raised to classic status by an exciting finale.

Access: There are no access restrictions.

'A' Climb (21.1), Ilkley

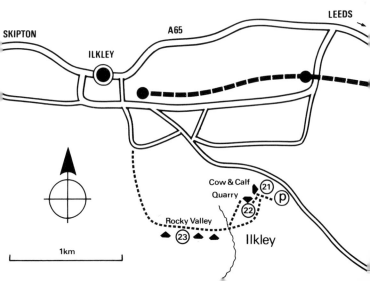

21: ILKLEY – COW AND CALF

Summary: A meandering classic and its exposed variant finish find unlikely ways up a forbidding buttress.

Crag Conditions: Faces north-east in an exposed moorland situation at 250m. However, the buttress is free of vegetation, takes little drainage, and so dries quickly. Though the rock is generally rough and solid, the footholds are highly polished.

Approach: From Ilkley town centre on the A65 between Leeds and Skipton, take the moor road following signs for 'Cow & Calf Rocks'. On arrival a track breaks off right to a large parking area just a few minutes from the crag (GR:131 468).

The Cow and Calf, a high buttress and its diminutive offspring, are the best known rocks at Ilkley. A line of hewn bucket steps, equivalent to a Scottish grade I winter route, ascends the slabby face of the Calf. The other sides of the boulder are rather more difficult. The smooth lower front face of the Cow is climbed only by The New Statesman (E8,7b) up the right arete, and by a nerve-racking, unprotected direct start to 'A' Climb – Cow Udder (HVS,5a). 'A' Climb, the classic of the buttress, creeps in from the left to a ledge above the smooth lower wall then exits via a tough groove or by the exposed alternative finish of Ferdinand. Either way involves about 30m of climbing, so at least one belay is usual.

21.1 'A' Climb (VD+) ✳ ✳ ✳
A wandering climb with an expeditionary flavour. Back-and-foot the chimney at the left side of the front face and overcome a boulder choke to enter a cave. Belay. Creep rightwards along the ledge onto the front face, climb a slim groove (runner), and step right onto a foot ledge leading to a belay below the roof. Struggle onto the block above, then enter a polished groove and climb it with a finger hold and other difficulties (crux) to the top.

21.2 Ferdinand (S+) ✳ ✳ ✳
An excellent, exposed finish to 'A' Climb. Fix a high runner under the roof above the second belay on 'A' Climb then continue the ledge traverse rightwards. Ascend the chiselled incuts of a polished slab (extremely exposed) to jams and runners in a crack at the right end of the overhang. Shuffle right then mantelshelf to gain an easier finishing slab.

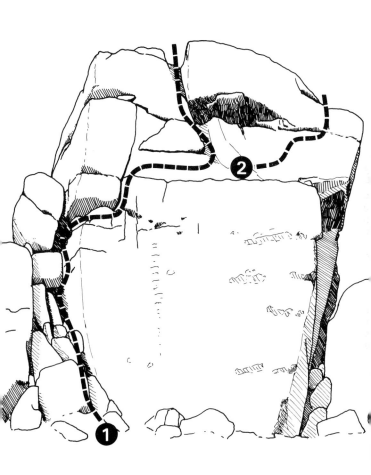

22: ILKLEY QUARRY – NORTH SIDE

Summary: A selection of popular quarry climbs, shorter and less fierce than usual of the type.

Crag Conditions: South-west fac ing and sheltered at an altitude of 250m. Dries relatively quickly, although some of the cracks carry drainage, and grit may be deposited on some holds. Despite the proximity of naturally outcropping grit, the quarry is very popular during sum- mer evenings and weekends.

Approach: Initially as for Section 21. Enter the quarry through the break in the short edge that extends to the left of the Cow and Calf.

Of the three walls in the quarry, the north wall is by far the most attractive. The face holds are typically square cut, while the cracks are sharp edged and ragged. The rock is intrinsically sound, yet even here, after many decades of use, friable flakes and suspect blocks are not unknown. Most routes are 12-15m in length. Top belays are better than usual at quarries, thanks to the jumble of natural boulders. The best descent is to the right of the wall.

22.1 Walewska (VS,4c) ✳ ✳ ✳
Ascends a devious line up the steep right-hand wall by some enjoyable climbing. Can be well protected. Start up a corner to the right of the main wall, exit left to a ledge, then go back right over bulges to a fine crack. A few moves up this lead to protection for a hand-traverse left, ending with a step down to a good foothold. A semi-mantel gains the friable flake cracks which provide a disconcertingly off-balance finish.

22.2 Josephine (S) ✳
Finds the easiest way up the wall. Begin up the right-hand and more prominent of twin cracks in the middle of the wall then move left above a semi-mantel to climb the left-hand crack, over blocks, to a foot ledge. Traverse the ledge leftwards and step awkwardly round into a niche (or step down and pull up into the niche) then use a good spike to swing left for a finish up the V-groove.

22.3 Josephine Superdirect (VS–,4b) ✳
Almost entirely independent of Josephine. Good, continuous climbing with no room for uncertainty. Directly beneath the final groove of Josephine is a shallow chimney cracked at both sides. The rock is polished and so a positive layback and/or bridging approach works best until good holds allow entry to a niche below a bulge (which can be avoided by stepping out right and entering the niche on Josephine). A good runner protects a strenuous pull over the bulge to the easy finishing groove of Josephine.

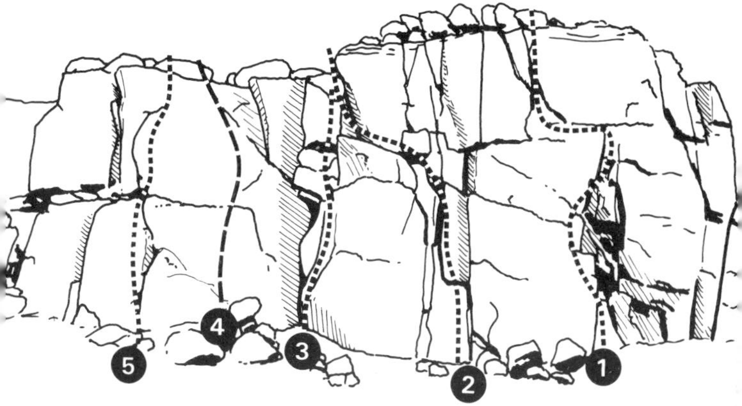

22.4 Fairy Steps (S) ✻

An unaccountably popular route which climbs the unprotected slabby wall to finish on the upper part of the ramp that slants across from the central break. Unprotected.

22.5 S Crack (VS,5a) ✻✻

A sustained thin crack climb near the left end of the Fairy Steps wall. Climb the slim, cracked groove (hard) and continue to the sandy break below the upper, curving crack. Step up to the right, then back left to reach the crack. A high step and long reach gain an excellent finishing hold.

23: ILKLEY – ROCKY VALLEY

Summary: Four middle-grade classics selected from the scattered buttresses of a pleasantly situated moorland outcrop.

Crag Conditions: The rocks face north-east at an altitude of 275m. Though set on the flank of a shallow valley, they are exposed to wind and bad weather and dry relatively slowly. When dry the rock gives good friction. Though popular enough, the Valley buttresses are generally quieter than the Quarry or Cow and Calf.

Approach: Initially as for Section 21. From the Cow and Calf, take the path passing left of the edge and go over the moor to the west, crossing a bouldery stream, to reach the depression which runs below the discontinuous line of buttresses. 10-15 minutes. Alternatively, from the Quarry base, scramble up the break at the left side of the back wall and walk south-west to the stream crossing.

Individually, none of the six Rocky Valley buttresses might warrant a special visit. Collectively they are the excuse for a lazy afternoon spent wandering down the Valley, bagging a route here and there. Here is just such a selection.

23.1 Stiction Chimney (D+) ✳ ✳

A protectable chimney which may or may not be climbed elegantly. Number Two Buttress is in fact two neighbouring crags: this 10m route splits the middle of the left-hand crag from bottom to top. A body-hugging V-chimney, not as easy as it looks, leads to the upper section which can be taken via a through-route or, harder, by climbing outside the chockstones (take a long sling for protection).

23.2 Flake Climb (S) ✳ ✳ ✳

This 15m route builds gradually to an exposed and exciting finish. Start at a pinnacle in the recess just right of the lowest point of Number Three Buttress. Step off the pinnacle and go over blocks into a cave. Ascend bulging rock to a large ledge on the left (alternatively, go up to the right to a good hand flake and swing left to the ledge). Monkey up the outside of the flake (big sling runner or fiddly nuts) then use mediocre wall holds to reach something more substantial for an exposed, high-stepping finish. Some care is required with top belays.

NUMBER TWO

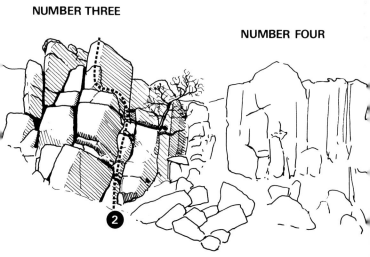

NUMBER THREE

NUMBER FOUR

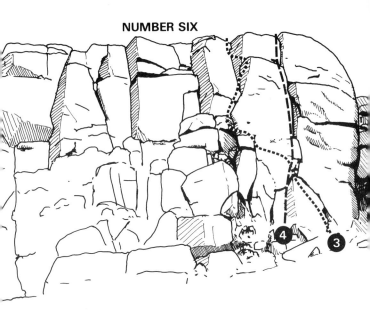

23.3 Spreadeagle (S+) ✳ ✳

This classic of Number Six Buttress, the most extensive of the Rocky Valley crags, weaves a 15m line up the right-hand side of the face in futile search of an easy exit. Start almost at the right edge of the buttress and climb a flake crack, trending left, to a small ledge. Short people now reach up for a good hand-traverse flake leading left, while tall people step left to a good foothold and then pull up. Either way a struggle ensues to get onto the block above. Now step left into the base of a big groove, bridge up (runner and, if you're not careful, rope drag), and mantel onto a ledge on the right. Step back into the groove for an easier finish.

23.4 Illegitimate Crack (VS−,4c) ✳ ✳

An excellent and well-protected direct line on Spreadeagle. Start up the Spreadeagle flake crack, or a slim groove to the left, to the small ledge. Jam up into a niche and stuff the crack with runners. When ready, jam the bulging and constricted crack (crux), helped by the wide crack in the right wall, to an easier finishing crack.

Flake Climb (23.2), Ilkley

Keighley and Heptonstall Moors

Yorkshire's western outcrops are found on or around the bleak moors extending into Lancashire. The three selected crags – Earl Crag, Heptonstall Quarry and Widdop – have their own devotees, but lie too far outside the main circle of crags to receive widespread attention.

Widdop, approached via a tortuous lane over the moor, is the most interesting of the three. Each of its main buttresses has its own distinctive character. Cave Buttress presents the familiar face of Yorkshire grit – bulging cracks brutally studded with flesh-gouging quartz crystals. If you can bear the pain, both Curving Crack and Cave Crack are excellent. Mystery Buttress, the largest at Widdop, is renowned for its extraordinary Ordinary Route – a gritstone oddity with an intestinal sense of direction. Purgatory Buttress is famous for, of all things, a blatant act of vandalism; the Artificial Route is just what its name implies. That this huge smooth slab, chipped into submission in the late 1940s, has been graded *VS+* should tell you something about the state of the pocket holds and of the frequency of protection.

Earl Crag has little appeal for outsiders. Set on the north-facing moor edge overlooking the town of Cowling, it often appears green and uninviting. Nevertheless, two of its middle grade climbs are undeniably classic – the daunting Earl Crack and the delightful Tiger Wall.

The attraction of Heptonstall Quarry is partly due to the charm of Heptonstall village, and of a pleasant woodland setting overlooking the Calder Valley. Graffiti on its walls is a reminder that some messages are important enough to be inscribed on tablets of stone (yes, but does Karen *still* love Colin?). Climbers are more humble: huge corners, leaning walls and poised blocks threaten all sorts of retribution on the over-imaginative mind. Under this sort of stress it is trial enough to creep up Fairy Steps, let alone struggle up Bull's Crack. Yet each is a must at its respective grade. As for that Whillans route, Forked Lightning Crack, most of us are content to stand and stare.

Access: At present there are no access restrictions to any of the selected crags. However, it is important to approach Earl Crag as described and not direct from the road below. Widdop is on water authority land so camping or bivvying is not allowed. Dogs should be kept on a lead or, better still, left at home.

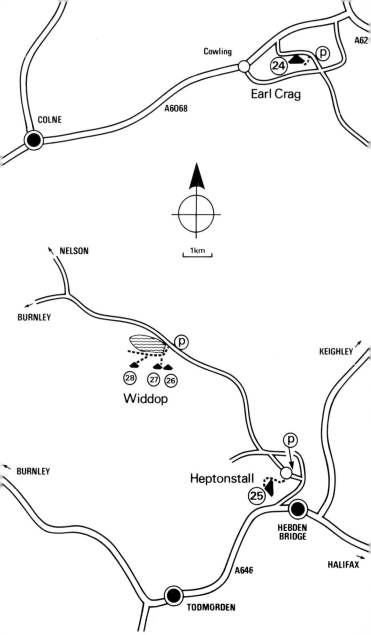

24: EARL CRAG – MAIN CRAG AND PROW BUTTRESS

Summary: A strenuous crack and an exhilarating face climb on an accessible yet generally neglected crag.

Crag Conditions: The crag faces north and dries slowly. However, the clean top of Prow Buttress promotes speedier drying.

Approach: Refer to access notes in the regional introduction. Approach via the A6068 between Colne and the A629 Skipton to Keighley road. At the eastern extremity of Cowling, turn south up the minor moor road towards Oakworth and follow it, rising below the crag, to a limited parking area where the road bends right to pass the east end of the crag. Follow the path through a quarry and over the meadow above the edge until within 100m of the pointed monument at the west end of the crag. Descend from here to arrive between Main Crag and Prow Buttress. GR:988 429. 10 minutes.

The 15m front face of the Main Crag can be climbed via the hanging crack and upper corner – Viscount's Route (HVS,5a); or by the right arete, gained from the start of Viscount's – Perch Wall (HVS,5b). Both are affected by the severely undercut base and by the interruption at two-thirds height from a vegetated bay. Earl Crack is unaffected by either feature and so provides the most continuous line. Prow Buttress is also undercut, but the 13m Tiger Wall succeeds in flanking the roof to find a feasible traverse line above.

24.1 Earl Crack (VS,4c) ❋ ❋ ❋
The impending corner crack on the right side of the buttress. The crack is wide and often greasy so stay outside. Only huge nuts will protect the lower part, but there's a good rest higher up from where to fix runners for the niche entry. The bulging final crack is awkward to start but soon eases.

24.2 Tiger Wall (S+) ❋ ❋
An exciting route which traverses the Prow above its roof. Technically reasonable, but requires careful ropework to protect the second. Start below the roof and trend left to a crack in the left wall (which could have been reached direct). Move up the crack and past a narrow ledge (runners), then traverse boldly right – good handholds but reachy – almost to the arete. Finish just left of the crest on excellent holds. Awkward belays well back.

MAIN CRAG

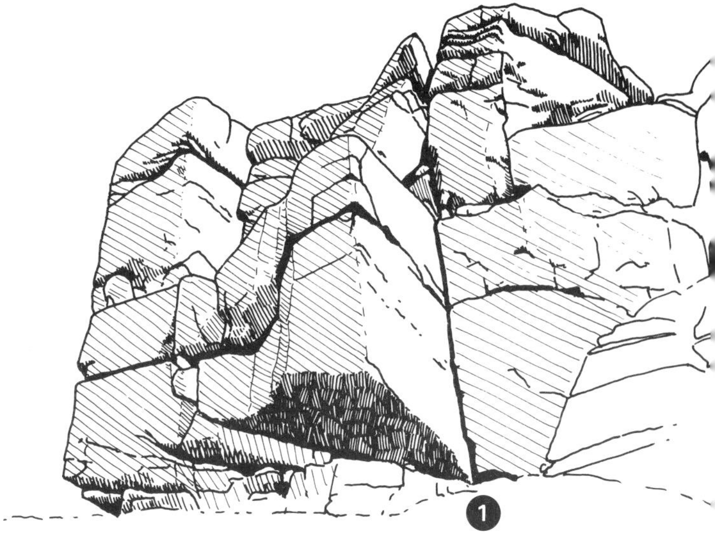

PROW BUTTRESS

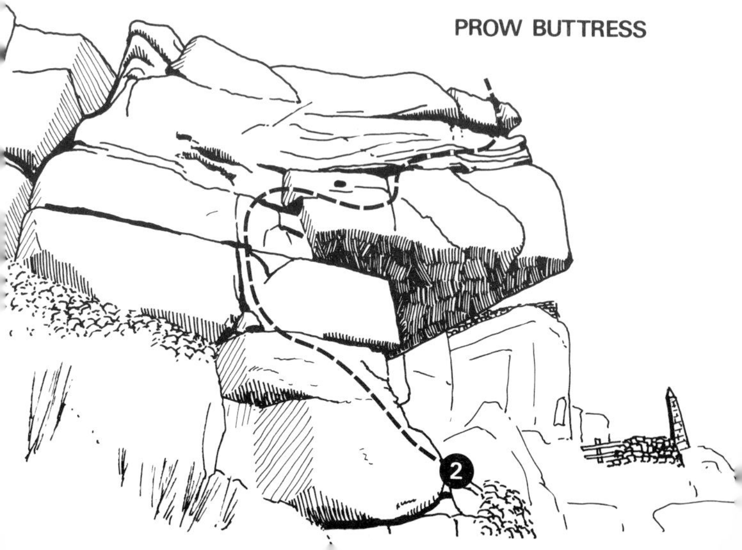

25: HEPTONSTALL QUARRY – YELLOW WALL

Summary: Two impressive climbs on the intimidating main wall of a secluded quarry.

Crag Conditions: The wall is set among trees in a south-west facing bay – a pleasant venue on fine winter afternoons and summer evenings. The overhanging nature of the rock keeps it dry during showers, although after prolonged rain it delivers drainage from the pasture above (Fairy Steps being most affected).

Approach: From the Todmorden (west) side of Hebden Bridge on the A646 Burnley to Halifax road, take the minor uphill road for Heptonstall (via the turning circle when approaching from Hebden Bridge), turning left shortly afterwards to enter the village itself. Car park on the right. Take the alley path between houses near the church (or, less atmospherically, a road through the housing estate) and follow the track marked 'Calderdale Way'. This soon narrows to a path between stone walls and finally zig-zags down steps to the huge boulder on the earthy rise opposite the Yellow Wall bay. GR:985 277. 10 minutes.

The 25m Yellow Wall is a recess in the main face: Fairy Steps follows a line based on the left corner (which can be climbed direct at VS,4c), while Bull's Crack takes the obvious line on the right. The series of stepped blocks left of Fairy Steps can be climbed to a traverse left and crack finish – Pulpit Route (VS,4c); and Rabbit Ledge gained via the overhanging and reachy right wall of Bull's Crack – Senility (HVS,5b). The infamous Forked Lightning Crack (E2,5c) follows the electrifying dogleg crack which splits the upper wall between the two described routes.

The yellow and black rock is of a blocky structure and less friable than some quarried grit. Nevertheless, there is always the possibility of a whole block becoming detached so a cautious approach is wise. Belays at the top are non-existent so stakes have been driven into the grass well back from the edge. With this in mind it is best to take a belay just below the top on both routes.

25.1 Fairy Steps (S+) ✳ ✳

An improbable route among the terraces, poised blocks and overhangs filling the left corner of the bay. Not technically hard, but with all the atmosphere of a big route. Protection is merely adequate. Start in the left corner below 'Rick', 'Lisa & Karl', 'Simple Minds' et al, and climb the corner crack until possible to move out right and up onto the first terrace (or climb the unprotected wall direct). Continue over ledges to a cave then trend left over stepped rock to a corner ledge. Traverse to the exposed left arete and climb via a mantel (side pull just right of the arete) to the top ledge and good belays. Traverse left and climb a short squeeze chimney to the top. Belay stake well back.

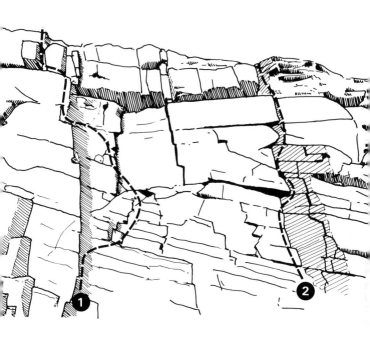

25.2 Bull's Crack (HVS,5a) ✽✽✽

A tremendous route up the gently overhanging corner at the right side of Yellow Wall. Large nuts required for protection in the lower crack. Jam and layback the first corner to the overhang (loose spike runner) then move onto good foot and finger edges on the right wall. With feet high in narrow slots, layback and jam over the right side of the overhang and continue up the corner to a swing right and mantel onto Rabbit Ledge. Climb the unprotected thrutch chimney above to a belay ledge just below the top. A final short chimney leads out onto grass (belay stake well back).

Fairy Steps (25.1), Heptonstall

26: WIDDOP – CAVE BUTTRESS

Summary: Twin *VS* crack climbs on the compact buttress of a moorland outcrop.

Crag Conditions: North facing at an altitude of 325m. The rock is often cold and greasy in the period from autumn to spring. Nevertheless, the buttresses take little drainage and there is no vegetation to retard drying.

Approach: Initially as for Section 25. Ignore the turn off into Heptonstall village and continue on the main road, later forking right (signposted 'Widdop') on the moor road towards Nelson and Burnley. Park on the verge near Widdop Reservoir and approach on foot via the dam road. Mystery Buttress rises ahead in line with the dam, Cave Buttress to its left. Purgatory Buttress, topped by a duck-shaped block, lies well to the right and is best approached by following the track on the far shore until a path branches left through boulders. GR:934 325. 10-15 minutes.

The front of the 14m high Cave Buttress is split by the leaning, cracked groove of Cave Crack. The thinner face crack which curves across the slightly overhanging wall to its left, joining the main line at the cave, is Curving Crack.

26.1 Cave Crack (VS,4c) ✷ ✷
The start is easier than it looks; the finish, harder. Bridge the beautiful starting corner and exit into the cave. Pull into the niche above and struggle up the exposed wide exit, probably facing left while wedging the right arm and shoulder.

26.2 Curving Crack (VS+,5a) ✷ ✷
A hard alternative start to go with the hard finish. The hand-ripping face crack leads to a half-rest at a horizontal break. When recovered, follow the slanting continuation, via a long reach to a rounded hold, into the cave.

27: WIDDOP – MYSTERY BUTTRESS

Summary: Meandering, low-grade climbs of great character in a moorland setting.

Crag Conditions: As for Section 26.

Approach: As for Section 26.

Mystery Buttress, 20m high showpiece of Widdop, is rare among gritstone outcrops in that its profusion of ledges add to, not detract from, the character of the climbs. The Ordinary Route wanders through this maze to give one of the more unusual gritstone *Diffs*. It is marred only by an anti-climactic finish – a criticism which cannot be levelled at Krypton Route when completed by one of its hard exit pitches.

27.1 Ordinary Route (VD) ✳ ✳ ✳

An episodic adventure. Most of the time is spent lurching from ledge to ledge. Good protection at the crux, but generally not otherwise. Step right from the large, flat-topped block at the foot of the front face and climb a crack trending left to Ledge 1. Move across to another ledge on the right (we'll call it Ledge 1.5 so as not to upset the traditional nomenclature). A protectable jam crack, or the wall to its left, then leads to Ledge 2 and, if required, a belay. Climb a flake crack up the slabby scoop on the right to Ledge 3. Crawl along the Stomach Traverse to a break in the bulge overlooking the rift on the right side of the buttress. Climb the break (crux), probably kneeling on the Bull's Horns in the process, to Ledge 4 and a belay. From a higher ledge (4.5?), traverse rightwards beneath overhangs to the easy exit chimney.

27.2 Krypton Route (VD+) ✳ ✳ ✳

A good companion route to the Ordinary, with optional hard finishes. Start near the right-hand toe of the buttress and climb up to the base of shallow, undercut groove (runners). Pull strenuously over the bulge and climb the elegant slim groove to a break. Ascend a slabby wall leftwards to Ledge 3 on the Ordinary. Pull straight up the short wall above (hidden hold over the top) onto Ledge 4. Belay. Three finishes are now available: (i) exit right as for the Ordinary Route; (ii) balance left in a very exposed position and layback The Flake (VS–,4b); or (iii) fist jam the short but brutal crack of The Layback (VS,5a) directly above the stance.

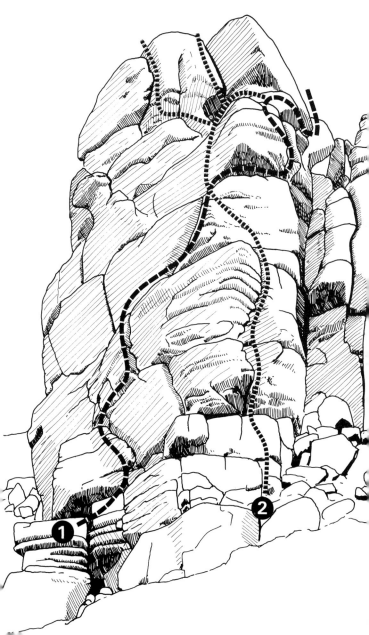

Krypton Route (27.2), Widdop

28: WIDDOP – PURGATORY BUTTRESS

Summary: A thrutch chimney and a chipped slab route on an outlying buttress.

Crag Conditions: As for Section 26.

Approach: Refer to Section 26.

The challenge of this compact 15m face proved so strong in the late 1940s that the Artificial Route was shamelessly chipped into existence. That it provides a good climb is no salute to the dastardly skills of the perpetrator.

28.1 Purgatory Chimney (VD+) ✲ ✲
A gallant struggle up the obvious, unprotected rift. Face left and thrutch, aided and abetted by a couple of chipped holds, then sit back for some conventional back-and-foot entertainment to a ledge near the top. Cross the gap to finish. The giant stone duck obliges with a belay.

28.2 Artificial Route (VS+,4c) ✲ ✲ ✲
A bold climb on inconveniently spaced, chiselled holds. Trend steadily left up the front face to a tiny ledge with runner possibilities. Follow chipped incuts up the shallow rib just right of the left arete to the overlap (runners). Pull out left on good flake handholds and ease over the top on more chipped incuts. Crack and duck belay.

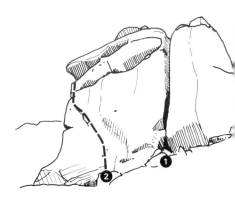

Chew Valley and Crowden Area

The northern limb of the Peak District encompasses Saddleworth Moor and Bleaklow. Encumbered by comfortless images evoked by those names, the region is shunned even by so-called gritstone enthusiasts. Excuses come easy: Wimberry is too hard: Laddow too easy: and Shining Clough too far. Why bother?

Wimberry is a crag for the gritstone connoisseur. Set on a boulder-studded slope high above Chew Brook, it offers little encouragement to the faint of heart. Before the recent crop of desperate wall climbs, it built a reputation on flesh-eating cracks. Freddie's Finale is one of these. But who wouldn't risk the odd scrape for the chance of succeeding on that other compelling Joe Brown route, The Trident?

As for Laddow, languishing above the empty valley of Crowden Great Brook, what possible interest could there be in a load of rambling *Diffs?* That's just it: the lack of widespread popularity *is* the interest. Those who come to climb at Laddow do so not simply to grapple with Long Climb or Tower Face (nothing *Diff* about that 5a problem entry), but to prolong time spent on the moor, out of sight and sound of towns, traffic and – for the most part – people.

No need to excuse Shining Clough. Though north facing and remote, perched on the northern fringe of Bleaklow, the quality of middle-grade climbs like Phoenix and Via Principia should be enough to lure the discerning gritstoner from Stanage. And if not, then the three-star classic of Pisa Superdirect surely will.

Access: There should be no difficulties provided the crags are approached as described. Dogs should be kept on a lead or, better still, left at home.

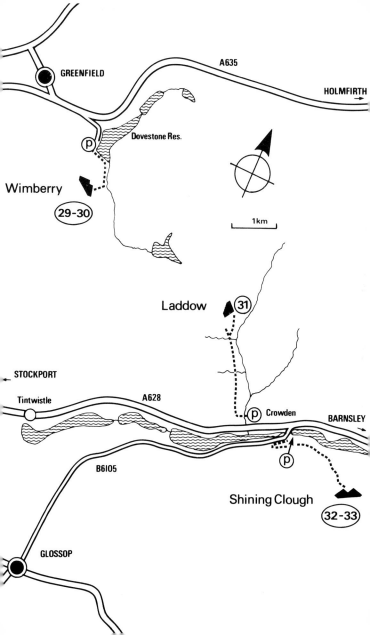

29: WIMBERRY – EAST SIDE

Summary: Corner and crack climbs of all grades on a major moorland outcrop.

Crag Conditions: North-east facing at 425m in an exposed situation. However, the crag top shelves back and thus limits drainage to the deep crack lines; the routes dry faster than you might expect, at least on breezy days. Although this is the best crag in the Chew Valley area, it is much less popular than even some inferior edges near Sheffield.

Approach: Take the A669 then A635 Holmfirth road out of Greenfield. Turn right on a minor road to Dovestone Reservoir (signposted 'Dovestone S.C.'), where there is a large car park (GR:014 035). Follow the track past the sailing club and around the south side of the reservoir. Turn right at a bridge and follow the stream bank to the Sugar Loaf boulder. Ascend direct up the steep hillside, yearning for other boulders on the way, to the left side of the crag (GR:017 024). 30 minutes.

Here, as on the west side, the big lines are blatant, uncompromising and very hard. Among these mighty features the slight Ornithologist's Corner is reduced to the status of filler, while even the cult route Freddie's Finale is grossly deflected by a blank wall. Overhang Chimney and Bertie's Bugbear are the nearest you'll get to an easy break here, which leaves The Trident as by far the most compelling climb in this selection. The three routes near the left side are 10-14m high, the two on the right, almost 20m. The usual descent is to the left of the crag.

29.1 Ornithologist's Corner (VS,4c) ✳ ✳
Neat, short, and benign. Good protection. Easy climbing leads to a ledge below the corner proper. Reasonable, if sustained, bridging leads to a strenuous jamming exit around the overhang.

29.2 Freddie's Finale (E1,5b) ✳ ✳
A nightmare of fist jamming and arm wedging. Good protection available from medium/large nuts deep in the crack, but few opportunities to place them. The initial overhang will see off all but the most determined, who will seek a moment's repose in the niche above before grunting up the appallingly off-width exit. Later, much later, the crack narrows to provide secure jams while feet find ripply support on the wall.

29.3 Overhang Chimney (VD) ✳
The chimney is undercut so start up its constricted depths and face left to get the feet above the overhang. With the crux over, and a thread coming, you can relax and enjoy the easing chimney and slabby corner above.

29.4 The Trident (HVS,5a) ✳✳✳

An attractive line, reminiscent of Curbar's Peapod in both appearance and solution. The pod itself is simple to enter but soon narrows and flares. Now every inch is hard won, mostly from vigorous application of back-and-knee with handjams at the rear of the crack for security. Assuming you are facing right (and one must sincerely hope that you are), you will eventually emerge below the Trident block itself, which is bridged with ease. The rest is simple.

29.5 Bertie's Bugbear (S) ✳✳

The deeply recessed V-groove. Protectable when it matters. Gain the initial easy corner direct, or sneak in from the right, and climb a wide crack to enter a steep groove (crux) which gives good jamming and bridging. Near the top, divert left at a block or finish direct.

30: WIMBERRY – WEST SIDE

Summary: A baffling chimney and a slabby corner provide good 'easy' ways up an otherwise unsympathetic crag.

Crag Conditions: As for Section 29.

Approach: As for Section 29.

The most obvious feature on the west side of the crag is the huge prow up which Appointment With Fear (E7,6b) finds its unlikely way. In its shadow the routes selected to left and right appear minor. This is not so. Route One, up the reclining corner to the right of the prow, has all the ingredients of a great route – line, quality of climbing, and a well-positioned crux. Starvation Chimney may lack quality of climbing but makes good with a puzzling bomb-bay exit. The major routes are over 15m long, the minor ones, in the vicinity of the usual scrambling descent down the break between Twin Cracks and Slab Climb, 10m or less.

30.1 Starvation Chimney (VD+) ✳ ✳
A treat for chimney freaks, climbing the apparently blocked rift to the left of the big prow. An easy entry to the wide fissure leads to an extremely smooth concave slab with an equally smooth leg crack to its right. The crack is a tempting option, but when the rock is dry it is better to friction up the slab to the blockage. The slot behind the block widens to normal body width only on the left, where there are no obvious means of effecting an entry. You might consider facing out, if you can bear the exposure, otherwise try facing in and cocking your left leg up.

30.2 Route One (S+) ✳ ✳ ✳
Quality climbing and a well-placed, protectable crux. Not to be missed. To the right of the big prow, and above a crevasse ledge at around mid height, is a recessed corner with a concave right wall. Gain the ledge by a straightforward wide crack then climb straight up the corner, initially by hand-jamming and foot friction, until the crack thins and closes at a thread. A long reach involving finger jams (crux) brings better holds at the exit.

30.3 Route Two (VS,5a) ✳ ✳
A worthwhile companion to the previous route. The main difficulties are concentrated in the first few metres. Climb the difficult wall right of Route One to get established in a finger crack leading to the crevasse ledge. Climb the slab and arete to a block and finish by a pleasant crack.

30.4 Twin Cracks (S+) ✳
A good jamming exercise in the left wall of the descent recess. Swing into the right-hand crack and jam it with conviction (purists will start lower down and struggle up the left-hand crack).

30.5 Slab Climb (VD+) ✳

Takes the left side of a clean slab, just right of a gully line, on the right side of the descent recess. Sustained and normally unprotected. Friction moves lead to a semi-mantel onto a sloping ledge on the left edge. The spell can be broken here by reaching into the gully to place protection for the crucial right-trending finish.

Route Two (30.3), Wimberry

The Trident (29.4), Wimberry

31: LADDOW – LONG CLIMB AND TOWER FACE AREA

Summary: A long approach to a remote crag rewarded by a selection of grip-and-pull classics.

Crag Conditions: The crag faces east at an altitude of 500m in an exposed situation. Pleasant on dry summer days, but not otherwise. Drainage can leave grit deposits on holds, though Long Climb and Tower Face are least affected. The long approach deters many, so the crag is usually quiet.

Approach: Via the A628 Stockport to Barnsley Road. From the large car park at Crowden (GR:072 993), follow signs for 'Pennine Way via Laddow Rocks'. Leave the path at the second major stream crossing, and just before it rises steeply, and contour rightwards to a level area of grass below the crag. GR:057 015. 1 hour.

Laddow lies back against the hillside and fails to impress, despite its respectable height of 15-20m (almost 30m in the case of Long Climb). Moreover, vertical features are obscured by the fine horizontal bedding. Requirements of a good route are therefore length and clean rock. Long Climb and Tower Face both qualify, while the two supporting routes can be used as an excuse to linger for another hour. The usual descent is to the right of the crag.

31.1 Long Climb (VD+) ✷ ✷ ✷
A mountaineering route in miniature. A slipped block provides the introductory pitch. Climb the slabby face of the block on polished holds to steep rock (runner), then step rightwards above the overlap and climb a crack to the commodious half-way stance. The upper section is quite different. Climb a steep but protectable crack to a niche and step left to a small ledge overlooking the gully. Finish up a slim, cracked corner in two stages.

31.2 Long Chimney Ridge (VD) ✷
Aims to climb the blunt arete right of Long Climb but succeeds in doing so only near the top. Start between the arete and the indistinct beginnings of Long Chimney and climb a subsidiary rib to a ledge. A short crack then leads to the Pulpit ledge (possible belay). Still on the right side of the arete, reach for a good hold above a bulge and make a gymnastic pull to get established at the base of twin cracks (crux). The cracks have good holds and protection and lead to a ledge on the arete. Climb a flake crack left of the arete then finish up the arete itself (loose block). Awkward belays.

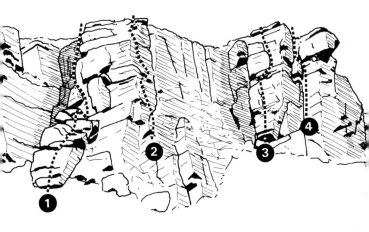

31.3 Tower Face (VS,5a) ✳ ✳

The clean rectangle of rock near the right side of the crag presents an obvious challenge. An infuriatingly difficult entry over the bulging base of the wall (using undercuts in pockets) leads to easier climbing and wire protection in a thin face crack. From the right end of the midway ledge, move right and up to another ledge to finish via a hand-width crack.

31.4 North Climb (D+) ✳

Climbs the big corner to the right of Tower Face. Atmospheric. Traverse into the corner from below Tower Face and climb the cone of slab that fills the base of the recess. The corner crack itself looks evil so climb the wide crack in the right wall – not without its own awkward moves – to an overhung ledge. An exposed foot traverse left (natural chock protection) leads into the corner proper, now a V-groove, which can be bridged to the top (alternatively make a difficult move up above the ledge before traversing left on good handholds into the corner).

32: SHINING CLOUGH – EAST BUTTRESS

Summary: A trio of middle-grade climbs based on the wide face cracks of a towering buttress.

Crag Conditions: Faces north at 450m on the fringe of Bleaklow, but being set into the hillside is partially sheltered. Both buttresses stand proud and so escape severe drainage. Via Principia and Pisa Super-direct catch the evening sun. The rock is more sheltered than usual for grit, the holds more square-cut, the cracks sharper edged. Loose blocks are not unknown. Despite good climbing, the long approach deters many.

Approach: As for Section 33.

Resolutely vertical, the East Buttress rises to 25m at its highest point. The front face is split by chimneys to far left and far right (the start of Via Principia), and by wide cracks to left and right of centre – Atherton Brothers and Phoenix respectively. Some care is required to find the best belays among the partially shattered rocks at the top of the buttress. Descend by collapsing ledges and a loose couloir to the left.

32.1 Atherton Brothers (S) ✳

An awkward climb with a dismal atmosphere; the least pleasant of the three. Protection is not always easy to arrange. Climb the flake crack – not as easy as it looks – to a good thread below the headwall. Move right – steep and suddenly exposed – and pull strenuously on good holds into the exit chimney. Scramble out or, more appropriately, finish outside the capping chockstone.

32.2 Phoenix (VS–,4b) ✳ ✳

Notable for the wide face crack early in the pitch, though the remainder is not without interest. Gain the crack directly on good flat holds. From an off-balance ledge, and protected by large nut runners, hand/fist jam past the distinctive pock-hole to reach excellent holds and a ledge above. Continue up a shallow chimney-crack and exit awkwardly onto a ledge. Move left to climb the final corner.

32.3 Via Principia (S) ✳ ✳

Enjoyable climbing up the west face of the East Buttress. The initial chimney-crack, steep but straightforward, leads to a ledge below its flaring continuation. This is not so inviting, so get out left and jam up a perfect crack near the arete, curving back right to a ledge above the chimney. Finish by a short wall.

Pisa Superdirect (33.1), Shining Clough

Phoenix (32.2), Shining Clough

33: SHINING CLOUGH – PISA BUTTRESS

Summary: An attractive buttress climbed direct up the front face by a magnificent *VS*.

Crag Conditions: As for Section 32.

Approach: Via the A628 Stockport to Barnsley road. Turn off at the Woodhead Reservoir on the B6105 to Glossop. Park at a sharp bend (GR:082 994) a few hundred metres from the junction. From about 500m down the road towards Glossop, turn left under the old railway on a gated private lane to Lodge Farm. Leave the lane at the 'no entry' sign to Lodge Farm and ascend the open hillside, later veering left to pass above a pool (stiles) and to cross a boulder-filled stream course. Resist the temptation to cut diagonally across the heather hillside and instead ascend the shoulder near the stream until a small contouring path leads left to the crag (GR:098 987). 45 minutes.

Pisa Buttress consists of an off-vertical right wall, a bulging arete, and a leaning left wall. The unattractive left wall is taken by the unsatisfactory Pisa and Pisa Direct routes, while the wide cracks on the right wall are linked by Stable Cracks. Pisa Superdirect takes the superb line up the buttress front between the two. Both described routes are about 18m long. As on the East Buttress, some care is required to get the best belays on top. The usual descent is by Deep Chimney – a loose gully to the right – at the base of which is a 5m pinnacle which can be climbed easily on its short side (D). The lower tier of the crag provides more short routes in the D-VS category.

33.1 Pisa Superdirect (VS+,4c) ✳ ✳ ✳
Exhilarating. Good protection. Climb a thin crack just left of the arete then move across to the right side and use a narrow-hand crack to gain a foot ledge on the right. Reach high and bridge wide (trusting a wobbly chock) to overcome bulging rock. The angle then relents, but the good climbing continues.

33.2 Stable Cracks (S+) ✳
Deceptive, and not easy to protect. An initial off-width sets the scene (though the trauma may be delayed by creeping in above it from the right), maintained by consistently awkward cracks above. Dogleg left for the smooth-sided crux, then finish easily.

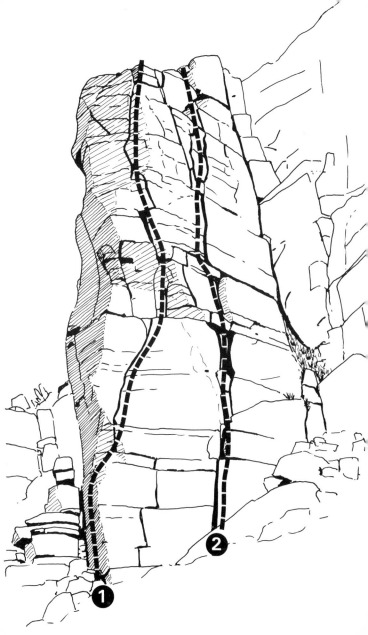

Kinder Scout and Edale Moor

The perimeter of the Kinder Scout plateau peels away into deep-cut valleys, in places revealing bits of the underlying gritstone. A string of these outcrops appears along the northern rim, while an odd collection of lumpy crags and dollopy boulders overlooks Edale on the southern rim. The northern crags are a little too esoteric for this tight selection, though a handful of routes from the southern outcrops have been included – the energetic Upper Tor Wall and the treacherously deceptive Herford's Route on The Pagoda among them. These routes can be combined in a circular walk from Edale by the climbing aesthete in possession of a pair of boots and a woolly jumper.

The bulk of routes in this section have been chosen from the crags of Kinder Downfall, where the River Kinder, having oozed out of the primordial gunge of the Kinder plateau, splutters over a rock barrier on its way valleyward (if it gushes not splutters you've chosen the wrong day). The Downfall Climb itself is the obvious target, though this is more of a curiosity than a climb. There are some good routes on the sprawling Great Buttress, but the real reward for this ninety minute approach are the climbs on The Amphitheatre. The name Great Chimney accurately portrays the route's presence, if not its character, while the name Zigzag Climb hints nothing of the romp to come up a wall of bucket-sized holds.

Access: There should be no difficulties provided the crags are approached as described. Dogs should be kept on a lead or, better still, left at home.

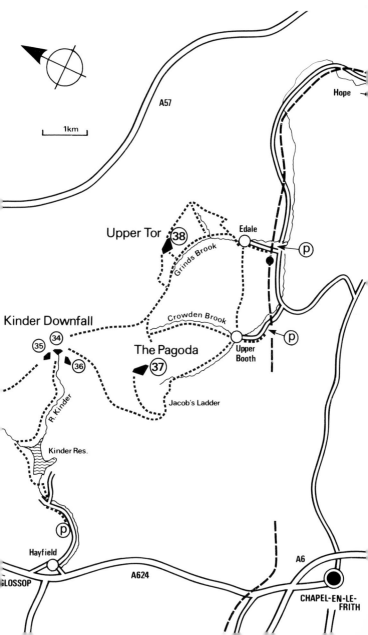

34: KINDER DOWNFALL – THE DOWNFALL

Summary: Technically uninspiring climbs elevated to classic status by a magnificent setting near the heart of Kinder Scout. Atmosphere is everything.

Crag Conditions: The Downfall, a rock barrier over which the River Kinder cascades, faces west at 550m. It is always wet. An exceptional summer may reduce the stream to a trickle, but expect the worst. South Corner takes no direct drainage but is often affected by the damp atmosphere. The long approach deters all but the most mountain minded of climbers. However, the rocks above the Downfall are a popular lunch stop for walkers crossing the plateau (some of whom are to blame for the drink cans, orange peel and other litter found stuffed among the boulders).

Approach: From Hayfield on the A624 Glossop to Chapel-en-le-Frith road. Turn off the main road for Hayfield village and continue on the minor road east to a car park in the quarry at Bowden Bridge (GR:048 869), appropriately the site where the original Kinder Trespassers gathered. Walk up the lane to the water authority gates, turn right and then, about 100m past the gates, leave the lane for a riverside path. At its end turn left to recross the river and pass through a swing gate just left of a second set of water authority gates. Follow the path high above the north side of the Kinder Reservoir. After crossing a bridge at the head of a deep inlet, ignore the main path, which goes straight on, and take a less distinct path on the right. This passes over a shoulder then descends to a ladder stile at the corner of a plantation. Follow the River Kinder upstream to the Downfall (GR:082 889). 1 hour 30 minutes.

The waterworn barrier of the Downfall is not a single high wall but a series of short ones interspersed with terraces and other transverse breaks. The Downfall Climb, all 35m of it, makes cunning use of these to climb an impressive piece of rock with a minimum of technical involvement, and is all the better for it. South Corner starts with the Downfall Climb at the right side of the barrier but then scuttles off up a more conventional chimney break to the right, reducing the length of climbing to 25m. With care, the Downfall Climb itself is the best descent. Otherwise descend cautiously between the Downfall and the Amphitheatre, or well beyond Great Buttress.

34.1 Downfall Climb (M) ✳ ✳
A unique, aquatic outing up the barrier waterfall of the River Kinder. Start at the corner at the right-hand side of the barrier and zig-zag up shelves on the left to the first terrace (or climb the corner direct to the same place at a similar standard). Make a long, rising traverse to the left along shelves and slanting

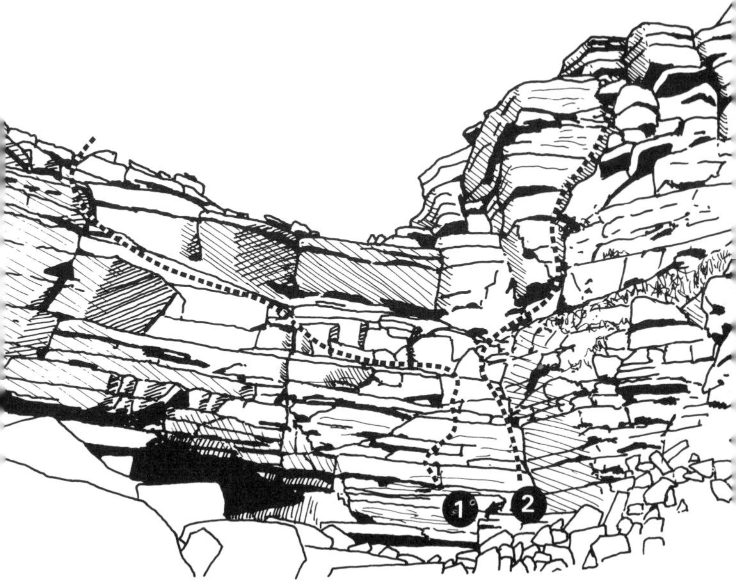

flake cracks (taking a shower as you go). Finish up the break at the left side of the barrier, probably dodging right at the final obstacle.

34.2 South Corner (VD) ✻

Drier and technically more interesting than the previous route but avoids the main issue. Start as for Downfall Climb and go up the corner and its continuation to a sandy cave. Pull over the cave roof and climb a shallow chimney to a grass ledge. Surmount a bulge to enter a wide crack and climb this, and its chimney continuation (via a through route), to the boulder maze at the top.

35: KINDER DOWNFALL – THE AMPHITHEATRE

Summary: Two great routes of contrasting character on the most remote of gritstone outcrops.

Crag Conditions: Refer to Section 34 for general remarks. The Amphitheatre faces south at 550m; however, the two central chimneys take some drainage and so can be gritty after rain. Great Chimney remains damp longer than Zigzag Climb, and must be absolutely dry for an ascent at this standard.

Approach: Initially as for Section 34. A bank of grass and loose rock guards the direct ascent to the Amphitheatre so approach diagonally left from the huge boulders below the Downfall.

The Amphitheatre is the most conventional of the Downfall buttresses, both in character and outlook. There are two bays: that on the right, composed of a curiously pocketed rock, is insignificant but for the high wall of Zigzag Climb at its left side; the larger, left-hand bay contains several chimney climbs. Route lengths are 15-18m. The best descent is down the back of the right-hand bay.

35.1 Zigzag Climb (D+) ✳ ✳ ✳

Exhilarating climbing up a near-vertical wall on huge holds. Start between the left arete and the chimney to its right and climb up on bucket holds. Gain a ledge on the arete by a flake crack. Step right on polished footholds and pull into a short, wide crack (crux). Exposed. A final confident pull brings the top within reach.

35.2 Left-Fork Chimney (D+) ✳

Start up the groove at the right-hand side of the bay then branch left at a ledge below its dirty continuation chimney for a slanting (crux) and shallow broken groove.

35.3 Professor's Chimney (D) ✳

Another 'filler', also liable to be gritty. Climb the break at the rear left side of the bay, initially by the chimney on the right then variously up cracks trending left.

35.4 Great Chimney (S) ✳ ✳ ✳

A memorable route, with plenty of technical interest. Protectable. Start at the foot of the right-hand groove and bridge up to reach a sharp-edged layback flake (protection). Use this to reach the square-cut, overhung recess. Swing left and mantel onto a small ledge below a slim corner (or step across high with a long reach into the corner). Climb the corner and easier continuation chimney to the top.

THE AMPHITHEATRE

GREAT BUTTRESS

THE DOWNFALL

36: KINDER DOWNFALL – GREAT BUTTRESS

Summary: Long, varied climbs overlooking the Kinder Downfall ravine.

Crag Conditions: Refer to Section 34 for general remarks. Faces west at 550m and dries comparatively slowly.

Approach: As for Section 34. Avoid the lower tier by traversing a narrow sheep walk leftwards below the main tier.

The 25m Central Chimney is based on the central recess; the 18m Great Slab on the slabby wall on the right-hand side. Descents immediately right or left are nerve-racking, so consider descending well to the right of all crags.

36.1 Central Chimney (D+ or VD+) ✳
Climb a grotty corner to a grass ledge below a square-cut chimney. Avoid a bulge on the right wall then step left and climb knobbly rock to a sandy cave. Escape left at D+ or arrange a soft heap of bodies and attempt the bomb-bay exit.

36.2 Great Slab (S) ✳ ✳
Good but not great. Also rather gritty. Start up the corner then climb a crack slanting across the right wall, deviating left to avoid a gritty exit onto the long ledge. Finish up the short wall. Care with belays at the top.

Herford's Route (37.3), Edale

37: EDALE – THE PAGODA

Summary: Deceptively awkward climbs on the rounded rock of an isolated buttress perched high on the rim of the Kinder plateau.

Crag Conditions: South-west facing at 625m. The rocks take no drainage and so despite their situation dry quickly during warm or breezy weather. Worth waiting for absolutely dry rock. Idyllic on a warm summer evening. Lots of walkers but few climbers.

Approach: (Refer also to Section 38 for a combined visit to The Pagoda and Upper Tor.) Approach via Chapel-en-le-Frith or Hope along the minor Edale road. Turn off for Upper Booth and park at GR:108 847, just after passing beneath the railway. Walk up the lane to Upper Booth. Shortly after the Edale path arrives from the right, the lane dips and bridges Crowden Brook. Now either (i) follow the path up Crowden Brook to the rim of the Kinder plateau and follow the path left, passing an area of natural rock sculptures, to the crag at GR:087 870 (hidden until the last moment during this approach); or (ii) continue up the lane and track and ascend by Jacob's Ladder to the Kinder plateau (as for the alternative Pennine Way route), before circling the rim rightwards to the crag. 1 hour 15 minutes by either route.

Wind and rain have eroded The Pagoda into the shape of a dollop of dough put to rise, the folds already blending into each other (though the rock texture remains extremely rough). Success depends on an exaggerated form of balance technique, so the routes are difficult to grade. Herford's has been graded *Severe* in the past, and yet some consider it *HVS*. The routes are longer than they appear – up to 20m.

37.1 Morrison's Route (S) ✳
A bit contrived, but a useful face-saver if defeated by Herford's. The most conventional of the three routes, and the best protected. Gain the terrace by a few energetic moves up an overhanging crack (4c to start), then, from its left end, climb the crack between the main face and the left-hand prow. Move left over a projection and go up to a boulder on the upper terrace. Finish left of the boulder with a long reach.

37.2 Hartley's Route (HVS,5b) ✳
Precarious climbing up the left side of the main face. Start as for the previous route to the first terrace, move right onto a flake, then mantel with difficulty onto a small ledge. Climb up past horizontal creases, making a hard move to reach the rounded edge of the top terrace. Step off the terrace boulder with a tricky move to gain a sloping ledge just below the top.

37.3 Herford's Route (VS+,5a) ❊ ❊

Looks to be of *Diff* standard and is anything but. Includes five cruxes, few of which are protected. Start below the main face, just right of centre, at a polished wall (the scratches rapidly diminish higher up). Jump for a letter box then move up and balance onto the first ledge using a flat hold and a mediocre pinch (or sneak in from the right). Thread on arrival. Slightly easier climbing leads up left past a horizontal crease (Friend) to a flared crack. Climb this via three sloping ledges, surmounted with increasing inelegance, to the top.

38: EDALE – UPPER TOR

Summary: Strenuous climbs on the well-weathered rock of a compact outcrop situated on the rim of the Kinder plateau.

Crag Conditions: South facing at 600m in an exposed setting. Pleasant on a calm, sunny day, but otherwise cold and bleak. The crag takes little drainage and so, despite its altitude, dries reasonably quickly. The path above the crag is popular with walkers, though the fairly long approach filters out most climbers.

Approach: From Chapel-en-le-Frith or Hope along the minor Edale road. Park near the junction of the no-through-road to Edale village (GR:123 853). Walk up the lane, passing through the village (parking here on quiet days), then fork right on the Pennine Way path, down steps and over the stream. Follow the path up Grinds Brook, veering left on the main path over the footbridge at the stream confluence, until below the crag, now visible high above on the right skyline. Either strike directly uphill, or continue until the path tops a mound of boulders and then ascend diagonally right to the crag. GR:113 876. 45 minutes.

Alternatively, incorporate Upper Tor with The Pagoda (Section 37) in a circular walk from Edale. In this case approach Upper Tor as above, then walk along the plateau rim westwards, past the indents of Grinds Brook and Crowden Brook, to The Pagoda, finally descending by the Jacob's Ladder route as described in the Section 37 approach.

Upper Tor has that melted look typical of moorland outcrops exposed to elemental sculpture. Rounded holds deny a security promised by rough rock, so a good technique will serve you better than strong arms. Nevertheless, the two described routes – unlike Herford's on The Pagoda – respond to the application of normal gritstone methods. Both ascend the left-hand and highest (18m) part of the crag: Upper Tor Wall on the left (west) side of the rounded arete; Hiker's Gully on the right. Harder variations on Hiker's Gully take the cracks and chimneys between its 'gully' line and the arete. The easiest descent is to the left of the crag.

38.1 Upper Tor Wall (VS–,4b) ✳ ✳ ✳
Varied climbing and a logical solution to the west wall. Steep, strenuous, and protectable (but take care to avoid rope drag). Start at a shallow cave at the foot of the arete on the right-hand side of the west wall. Surmount a short, overhanging wall left of the cave to enter a sentry box then pull awkwardly left onto a ledge. Spirited laybacking up the overhanging flake crack leads to a short, wide crack and a ledge. Jam out rightwards under the overlap to get onto a higher ledge and finish up a short crack.

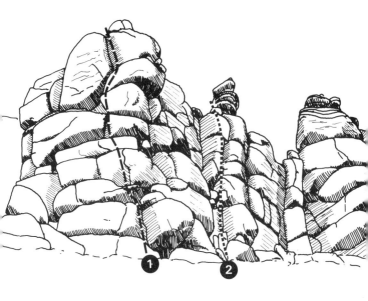

38.2 Hiker's Gully (D+) ✳✳

Not much to do with gullies (nor with hikers, for that matter), but with a series of cracks and chimneys. Strenuous and sustained. A pillar separates a crack on the left from a greasy chimney on the right. Start up the crack and make a difficult pull (good thread runner) to a ledge. Move up rightwards to the base of a wide, shallow chimney. Pull up to good holds on the left then bridge the exit with a determined finish over rounded blocks.

Goyt Valley Area

The Peak District National Park boundary doubles back at Buxton and loops across towards Macclesfield to include a node of scenic upland surrounding the Goyt Valley. The map shows a clutter of picnic sites, viewpoints and forest trails. And also the tell-tale spidery symbols of gritstone edges at Castle Naze and Windgather.

At Windgather you will see – when you can see anything at all behind the swarming bodies of eager and not so eager young people from nearby schools and outdoor centres – a crag set at the optimum height and angle for those first steps on grit. Such is the profusion of holds that an indecisive climber may never get off the ground. Roped or solo, an afternoon spent here is the rock climbing version of occupational therapy; no-one pretends that it stimulates the mind, but it's ideal for loosening up the fingers. There is no such thing as a classic climb at Windgather; it is the crag as a whole which is classic.

Castle Naze, tucked away on a little hill of its own, is often mistaken for a substitute Windgather. True, most of the climbs are short and in the lower grades, but there the similarity ends. There is no surfeit of holds here, and good belay anchors at the top are scarce. Imperfections of both rope and climbing technique will be ruthlessly exposed. Nevertheless, a dozen good climbs at *V.Diff* and *Severe* await the basically competent, while the more accomplished climber can enjoy the balance moves of Scoop Face and the secure jams of The Crack, both of an approachable *VS* standard.

Access: There are no access restrictions at present provided the crags are approached as described. Dogs should be kept on a lead or, better still, left at home.

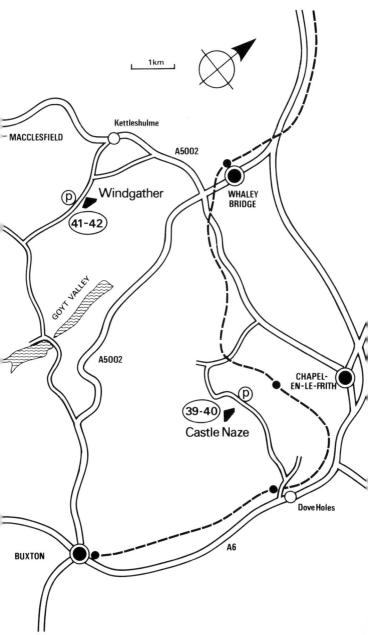

39: CASTLE NAZE – LEFT-HAND SECTION

Summary: A large selection of low-to-middle grade routes on a short, compact and accessible outcrop.

Crag Conditions: West facing at 425m. The crag takes only a moderate amount of drainage so most routes dry quickly after rain. Much less popular than Windgather, though many of the holds are nonetheless highly polished.

Approach: Via the A6 Chapel-en-le-Frith to Buxton road. At Dove Holes, turn off (west) on a minor road past the railway station, then turn left on Cowlow Lane. Just before the road starts to descend steeply, there is a layby on the left with room for 3 cars. The crag is on the hillside above but not yet fully in view. From a gate and stile 50m back up the road, follow a path diagonally across the hillside to the crag at GR:052 784, less than five minutes away. Do not approach via the track signposted to Castle Naze Farm.

A bouldery descent corner divides the crag into two distinct sections: a short, attractive left-hand section cut by numerous crack, chimney and arete lines; and a much larger but generally loose and uninviting right-hand section on which only those routes on The Tower at its left side have been described (along with, for convenience, routes in the Scoop Face area). Though the rock is more square-cut than at Windgather, the holds are further apart. So despite a length of only 8-10m these are tough little routes. The top of the crag shelves back in shattered layers where belay anchors are difficult to arrange. Patience and plenty of rope are the answer.

39.1 Nithin (VD+) ✳
Start up a cracked corner just left of the arete (hard) then climb the arete to a ledge at half height. Finish more easily up the chimney on the left. A good alternative approach is by the leaning wall to the right of the arete.

39.2 Flywalk (VD+) ✳
Climb the crack in the right wall of the big corner, initially by wide bridging, then step left onto a large ledge for an easier finish trending right. Protectable.

39.3 Niche (S) ✳
Climb the lower crack to the niche and surmount it energetically. Continue up the flake crack, trending right to an easy finish. The arete to the right gives a good, problematical approach to the niche.

39.4 Studio (S) ✳
A thin crack just left of the arete gives a hard but protectable approach to a small ledge. Finish more easily up the left-trending twin cracks above.

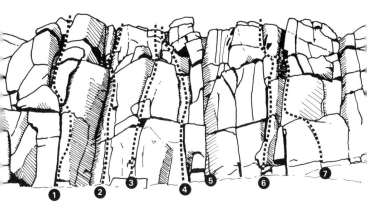

39.5 AP Chimney (S+) ✳

Climb the wide corner crack with few runners and no respite to the chock.

39.6 Pilgrim's Progress (S+) ✳

Enter the pygmy-sized sentry box then jam up the crack above. Quit the crack where it widens and slants left to climb the bold arete to a ledge. Finish up the corner with an awkward exit.

39.7 Little Pillar (VD+) ✳

Climb the shallow groove in the middle of the wall (hard to start) to a ledge. Go up the corner then exit left at a ledge and finish awkwardly up the corner of Pilgrim's Progress.

40: CASTLE NAZE – THE SCOOP AND THE TOWER

Summary: More short climbs in the lower grades, plus two minor *VS* classics.

Crag Conditions: As for Section 39.

Approach: As for Section 39.

The route up the front face of The Tower contrasts with the superb delicacy of Scoop Face. Again the routes are 8-10m in length. Belays are good above The Tower, though not above Scoop Face. Descend by scrambling down the broken corner between Scoop Face and The Tower.

40.1 Keep Corner (S) ✳
Climb the corner left of Scoop Face with some awkward bridging to finish. Harder than it looks, but the protection is good.

40.2 Keep Arete (S+) ✳
The left edge of Scoop Face. Climb the serious lower arete with a move right at half height. Improving handholds compensate for diminishing footholds as the half-height ledge approaches. The upper arete is exposed but protectable.

40.3 Scoop Face (VS,4b) ✳ ✳
Delightful climbing. Technically reasonable but protection is scarce. Start at the left arete and at once trend right on creases to gain the Scoop. Continue rightwards across the polished slab then step up to a pocket and large nut runner. Pull up to get established on the ledge on the left then finish direct on pinches. (A 5a direct start enters the left side of the Scoop on sloping holds.)

40.4 Footstool (D+) ✳
Climb the second break to the right of Scoop Face on good holds, initially by a flake crack to a ledge, then by a more broken corner.

40.5 Deep Chimney (D) ✳
The deep fissure between the descent route and The Tower.

40.6 The Crack (VS−,4b) ✳ ✳
A miniature classic, well protected and not too polished. Balance up the cracked lower wall to a shelf below the crack proper. Bridge up to the overhang and jam over it to good holds, more runners and – too soon – the top.

40.7 Long Climb (D) ✳
Length is its main merit. Climb the corner on the right of The Tower to a rock-littered shelf then finish up the break in the left wall.

THE SCOOP

THE TOWER

41: WINDGATHER – NORTH AND MIDDLE BUTTRESSES

Summary: Ideal climbs for beginners on a friendly, accessible outcrop.

Crag Conditions: West facing at 400m. Dries quickly. Very pleasant on a sunny afternoon or evening. Often crowded with groups of young people from schools and outdoor centres.

Approach: Via the A5002 Whaley Bridge to Macclesfield road. Turn off at the south end of Kettleshulme village on the minor uphill road. Follow it for 2km/1 mile to layby parking for several cars a few minutes from the crag. GR:995 783.

The rocks are grouped in a continuous edge 5-8m high punctuated at intervals by prominent buttresses; only these longer routes (10m) have been described. Most of the rock lies back at an amenable angle and is liberally covered with good holds, many of them highly polished. Top belay anchors – like the runners – are generally good, though not always immediately obvious.

41.1 North Buttress Crack (M) ✳
The prominent cracked corner.

41.2 Green Crack (VD+) ✳
Climb the recess to a polished scoop then bridge up right and climb the leaning crack on good holds.

41.3 North Buttress Arete (D+) ✳
Get onto the ledge on the right, enter a niche above, then move left onto a ledge on the arete. Step left onto the face and finish on good holds. Alternatively, approach the arete ledge direct (S).

41.4 Wall Climb (D) ✳
The left-trending line leads without complication to the leaning exit slot, which feels serious but has good holds and is protectable.

41.5 Central Route (VD) ✳
A devious route up the central wall, finishing up a thin crack. Good moves but elusive protection.

41.6 Chockstone Chimney (D) ✳
Not a chimney at all but a slight, left-leaning crack gradually widening to arm width. Protectable.

41.7 Mississippi Crack (VD) ✳
Ascend the thin crack in the middle of the face, with wall climbing to start and finish.

41.8 Middle Buttress Arete (D) ✳
Climb up just left of the arete to a ledge. Step left onto the exposed upper arete and follow it on good holds to the top.

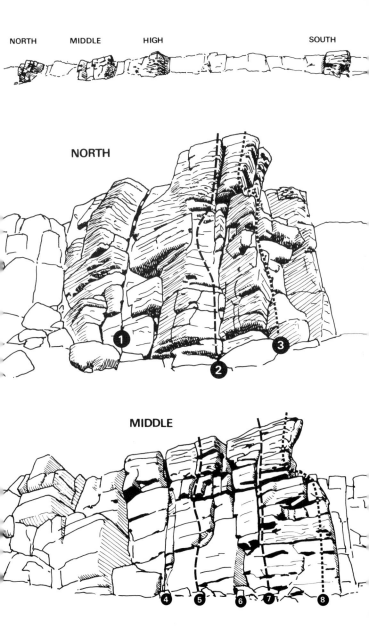

NORTH   MIDDLE   HIGH   SOUTH

NORTH

MIDDLE

42: WINDGATHER – HIGH AND SOUTH BUTTRESSES

Summary: Ideal climbs for beginners on a friendly, accessible outcrop, plus a couple of harder problems on steep rock.

Crag Conditions: As for Section 41.

Approach: As for Section 41.

Refer to Section 41 diagram for location of buttresses.

42.1 High Buttress Arete (D) ✳
Climb an intermittent crack-line on the right-hand side of the arete, then move left to a ledge and finish up the arete on good holds.

42.2 High Buttress Direct (VD+) ✳ ✳
Start 2m left of the arete and climb straight up to the ledge of the normal route.

42.3 Route Two (VD+) ✳
Get onto the block, swing rightwards across the overhang, then pull back left into the crack to finish.

42.4 Route One (VS,5a) ✳
Enter the shallow cave, pull up left on the overhanging wall, and then make an unprotected and committing move for a good hold above. Continue up the leaning wall on flat holds to an easy finish.

42.5 South Buttress Crack (M) ✳
The pleasant corner crack.

HIGH

SOUTH

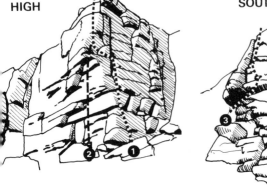

Route One (42.4), Windgather

Ladybower and North-East Area

Divisions between town and country blur beyond the north-east boundary of the Peak District National Park, where electricity pylons bushwhack through bracken and boulders below Wharncliffe Crags. This is townified country. Disparaging remarks about the rock – a blackened and frequently lichenous fine-grained grit – have effectively deterred outsiders. In fact the rock is pleasant to climb, and gentle on the hands after a couple of days spent on authentic hand-ripping stuff. The classics here are minor ones, among which Himmelswillen stands out.

Nearer to Sheffield, but narrowly included in the park boundary, Rivelin Edge enjoys a similar neglect from outsiders. Shy behind trees, the edge thrusts forward the Rivelin Needle as its main attraction. The direct Croton Oil and the convoluted Spiral Route, enjoyable enough in themselves, are terrific as means of reaching the summit of this otherwise inaccessible pinnacle.

Some of the character of Bleaklow and Kinder extends eastwards, beyond the dammed upper reaches of the River Derwent, onto the Derwent Moors. Derwent Edge is the backbone of the moor, and its main highway. There are many more walkers here than climbers, despite scattered lumps of grit and the large outcropping of Dovestone Tor on the windswept crest high above the Ladybower Reservoir. In fact you can't be a climber here without also being a walker of sorts, or at least receptive to its rewards. Great Buttress would be a great route anywhere. In this setting it is magnificent.

Bamford Edge lines the hilltop above the lower Ladybower Reservoir and has more in common with Stanage than Dovestone Tor. Access restrictions and the proximity of Stanage ensure that few climbers bother to come here, yet for those who do there is a clutch of excellent middle-grade routes based on aretes and cracks, among which Neb Buttress and Brown's Crack are outstanding.

Access: Three crags in this region lie on private land and are subject to access restrictions:

- Climbing at Wharncliffe is allowed, but officially only on Mondays, Thursdays, Saturdays and Bank Holidays.
- Climbing on Rivelin by considerate parties is allowed provided the crag is approached as described.
- Bamford Edge lies on a grouse moor with no right of access. Nevertheless, small groups are generally allowed to climb here during the period October to March, provided they first contact the keeper Mr F. Darwent (Tel: Hope Valley 51458).

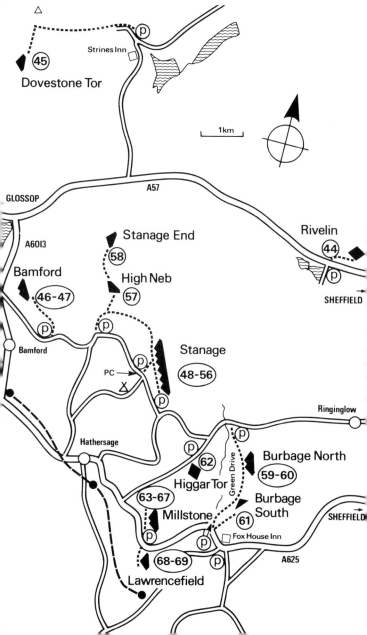

43: WHARNCLIFFE – HELL GATE AREA

Summary: A small selection of low and middle grade routes on unusually fine-grained gritstone.

Crag Conditions: South-west facing at 250m. Takes little drainage and so dries quickly. Holds seem to be either lichenous or polished, so it's worth waiting for dry rock. An un-fashionable edge, and therefore relatively quiet, though a convenient evening venue for local climbers in summer.

Approach: Refer to access notes in the regional introduction. Approach via the A616 Sheffield to Stocksbridge road. When arriving from the Sheffield side, turn right at the Deepcar (east) end of Stocksbridge on the B6088. After a hundred metres or so, turn right again on Station Road. Roadside parking after 300m near the Lowood Club (GR:292 982). Soon after bridging the river, turn left on a footpath up a sandy bank, later merging with a track. Veer right from the track after 10m and squelch under the railway to rejoin the now cobbled track (bring your wellies or follow the track throughout over the railway sidings). After passing to the left of a pool, the track degenerates to a path, goes through a second, drier tunnel and then comes to the Plank Gate track. Cross it 10m to the left and continue on an uphill path to a lake. Fork right here (initially not obvious) and follow a path rising along the crest of the edge. Continue until within 60m of a collapsed stone wall at right-angles to the crag (and beyond which the path levels and the crag begins to fizzle out). Hell Gate buttress now lies below. GR:296 975. 25 minutes.

Though extensive, Wharncliffe is generally low and of limited interest. The Hell Gate area is relatively high (10-12m) and includes the classic *VS* of the crag. The rock is a fine-grained grit, providing more flat holds but fewer jam cracks than coarse-grained grit. It offers good friction but is vulnerable to polishing, and might be compared to well-weathered quarried grit. Descend to left or right, or between the two buttresses.

43.1 Himmelswillen (VS,4c) ✳ ✳
Steeper than it looks, and therefore unexpectedly difficult. Adequately protected. Gain a ledge on the left edge then traverse rightwards under the overhang to a flake crack. Semi-layback the crack (crux) to a good horizontal handhold then step left onto a ledge. Ignore the thin crack on the right and finish near the left edge on surprising holds.

43.2 Teufelsweg (D) ✳
The big cleft. After a tricky start, or a walk in from the right, bridge up with protection possibilities to finish outside the top chock.

43.3 Tower Face (S+) ✳

Climbs the narrow face of the tower 25m right of Himmelswillen. Mostly straightforward, but with a technical crux at half height. Start up the wide fissure then get onto the concave slab on the right (probably by devious means). After placing runners in the thin crack, climb the right edge to better holds and an easing finish.

43.4 Hell Gate (VD) ✳

Employs the full repertoire of inelegant gritstone techniques – including knee work, squirming and mantelling – to get from one ledge to another in the left-hand corner line of Hell Gate Buttress.

43.5 Hell Gate Crack (S) ✳

The flake crack on the front wall of the buttress. Gain the crack awkwardly and climb it to the bulge. Swing right and semi-layback to the birch tree. Traverse a slot rightwards and grovel up into a recess. Exit ignominiously or step left and climb the top wall.

Himmelswillen (43.1), Wharncliffe

44: RIVELIN – THE NEEDLE

Summary: A free-standing pinnacle, its summit unattainable at less than *VS*, climbed by two excellent and contrasting routes.

Crag Conditions: Generally south facing at 250m (the Spiral Route also visits north and west faces of the Needle). Trees shroud the edge so dampness (and midges in spring and summer) will linger after rain on calm days. All faces of the Needle dry quickly if there's a breeze. The crag is not widely popular with outsiders, though being close to Sheffield it may be busy on fine summer evenings.

Approach: Refer to access notes in the regional introduction. Approach via the A57 Sheffield to Glossop road. There is severely limited roadside parking near the Rivelin Dam (GR:276 869), on the Sheffield side of the Norfolk Arms (possible alternative parking). Take the signed footpath opposite the junction of the dam road and follow it through trees, later contouring right to enter birch woods. Turn left on a lesser path marked 'Access for rock climbers only' which later divides. The crag is hidden by trees, but on arrival by either path you probably need to traverse right to find the Needle. You'll know when you get there. GR:280 873. 10 minutes.

The Rivelin Needle is a famous gritstone challenge, the easiest way up being the circumnavigatory Spiral Route, which starts on the South Face, belays on the North Face, and traverses the West Face before finding itself on the South Face again, only a few metres higher but in a position to mount a summit bid. Croton Oil scorns such diversionary tactics and climbs straight up the South Face, at 15m the highest on the Needle. If reversing Spiral Route does not appeal, which is likely, then the only feasible descent is by abseiling down the short North Face from a small block on the east side of the summit (in which a groove has been cut to help secure the rope). This can be backed up with threads if required.

A couple of routes have been described from the many on the 10-14m high main edge behind the Needle. The quickest descent from either of these is down the back of the bay behind the Needle (very awkward near the bottom).

44.1 Spiral Route (VS,4c) ✳ ✳
Aims to get to the summit of the Needle by the easiest route possible, and succeeds. Not technically hard but intimidating. Double ropes useful for protecting the second. Climb the narrow-hand crack above a ledge near the right side of the South Face – steep but with good holds and protection – to the big ledge. Belay. Above the far right-hand side of the ledge, a horizontal crack can be reached at full stretch (runners). Step up on small footholds and launch off around the right arete on good holds, suddenly exposed, and onto

the North-West Face. More horizontal holds and jams, and a sloping but sufficient foothold, allow a longish reach right to an improving part of the crack and the wherewithal to get stood up on the Notch – a ledge on the arete between the West Face and South Face. Above is the friable flake finish. A good runner above the hollow section protects a difficult move (inevitable if the suspect flake is to be avoided) to better holds and the top. Belay on the abseil block/threads with a directional back-up in a crack in line with the finish.

44.2 Croton Oil (HVS,5a) ✳ ✳ ✳

A direct and enjoyable ascent of the Needle. It links, by a series of intricate moves, the ledge at one-third height on the South Face with the Notch, a ledge at two-thirds height on the arete between the South Face and West Face. Neither strenuous nor excessively difficult, but requires the confidence to make committing moves beyond protection. Layback the rounded edge of a wide flake crack to the first ledge and follow a right-trending crack to a horizontal crease (runners). Move boldly up and left, via a vertical finger slot and then a better finger crack (good runner), to a good flake crack leading to the Notch. Finish via the suspect flake crack as for Spiral Route.

44.3 Blizzard Ridge (HVS,5a) ✳ ✳

Excellent balance climbing up the left-bounding arete of the bay behind the Needle, marred only by escape possibilities at half height. Protected by fiddly and spaced runners. A problem start up the right-hand side of the blunt arete leads to better holds and balancy moves up and left onto a small ledge. Ascend to ledges on the left side of the arete then move up and right, on mediocre holds, onto the edge (crux). Transfer to the right side of the arete at the overlap and surmount it using undercut pinches and a high step. Better holds arrive near the top. Belay anchors are a long way back, either at the fence or well over to the right.

44.4 David's Chimney (D+) ✳ ✳

Climb the open, cracked groove at the left side of the bay behind the Needle, ending at a birch tree. Reachy to start and finish.

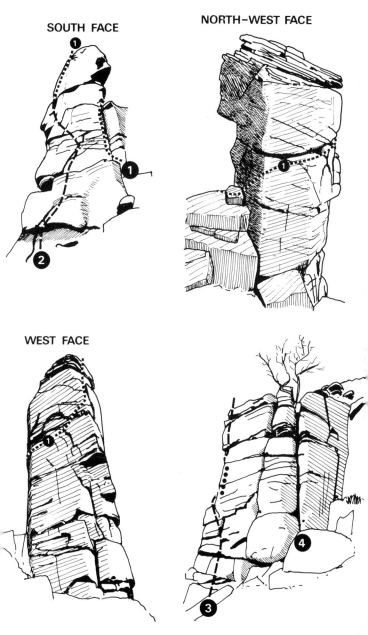

SOUTH FACE

NORTH-WEST FACE

WEST FACE

45: DERWENT EDGE – DOVESTONE TOR

Summary: A high, remote and intimidating moorland outcrop.

Crag Conditions: West facing at 500m in a very exposed situation. The rock is rough but lichenous, so worth waiting for dry weather. The top of the edge is popular with walkers, though the long approach deters most climbers.

Approach: Via the A57 Sheffield to Glossop road. From 3km/2 miles east of the Ladybower Reservoir, follow the minor road north, passing the Strines Inn after about 3km/2 miles, to where the descending road bends sharp right. Park where a surfaced lane branches left (GR:221 909). Walk up the lane to a gate (15 minutes). Continue parallel to the stream on a broad path, rising steadily across the moor. Turn left at the crest and follow the path along the broad top of the edge. Before reaching the Cakes of Bread, branch right towards the obvious buttress profiled on the right. GR:196 897. 1 hour.

The aptly named 20m Great Buttress is riddled with pock-holes and layered with overhangs. The left side of the main wall has more pock-holes than overhangs, so this is where Dovestone Wall and Brown Windsor find a way through. The right side is severely undercut by a large cave and topped by a roof. Great Buttress escapes the cave and flanks the roof with some spectacular climbing. Route One climbs the much smaller (10-12m) prow-topped buttress 50m to the right of the cave. The rock is brutally rough, and thankfully there is little need for jamming. Descend by an easy scramble to the right of Great Buttress.

45.1 Dovestone Wall (D+) ✳
Of little intrinsic interest, though the setting is impressive. Start just right of the gully and zig-zag up the easing wall looking for large holds and protection. Step awkwardly left to flank the top overhang.

45.2 Brown Windsor (VS,4b) ✳✳
A good face-saver if Great Buttress proves too much. Start left of the main undercut and gain the right end of a ledge below a thread pillar. Trend right then go straight up, past a hard pull over an overhang into a niche (crux). Trend left on good holds beneath the big roof and pull over the bulge at its left end to finish up an easy slab.

45.3 Great Buttress (HVS,5a) ✳✳✳
Most of the climbing takes place on huge holds, but the crux comes at the top when muscles and nerves are taut. Good protection, but spare a thought for rope drag (and for the second). Pull up the left wall of the cave and traverse to a niche round the arete. Pull into a higher niche then climb over bulges on

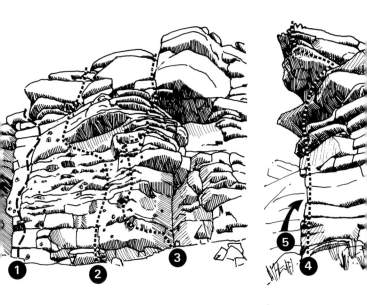

good holds. Before strength ebbs away, traverse right in an impressive position to a cracked block (runners and semi-rest). Ascend the bulging wall with conviction and paw over the top on rounded holds. Good thread belay on the right. Struggle up corners above the thread to finish (or walk left to escape via Brown Windsor).

45.4 Route One (VS,4c) ✳ ✳
Climb the arete via three, thought-provoking mantels. Now either creep off to the right via the ordinary finish or, for the Shylock Finish, deposit your pound of flesh in the lowest break leading left onto the prow and finish over the crenellated tip.

45.5 Wind Tunnel (M) ✳
The rift to the left of the prow of Route One. A good descent from that route, but worthwhile in itself.

46: BAMFORD EDGE – NEB BUTTRESS

Summary: A large buttress in a pleasant upland setting, providing an easy cleft, a wall climb and two hard aretes.

Crag Conditions: South-west facing at 400m. Exposed to bad weather but pleasant at other times. Access restrictions and the proximity of Stanage limit numbers at the crag.

Approach: Refer to access notes in the regional introduction. Turn off the A57 Sheffield to Glossop road at the Ladybower Reservoir on the A6013 to Bamford. 1.5km/1 mile from the junction, and 200m past the Yorkshire Bridge hotel, turn left up a minor road signposted to Bamford Moor (refer to the map for other approaches). The road rises steeply and the crag is visible high up on the left. Limited roadside parking at GR:216 839 where the incline eases (iron gate on left and stone ruin nearby in field). Don't head towards rocks visible on the left but ascend the hill directly towards the ridge then trend left on a narrow path. The first crags above the path are those of The Gun area (Gun Buttress, identified by its eponymous neb, contains three *VS* routes based on the undercut crack on the right, the front face, and the left-hand face). 50m further on, a subsidiary path descends to below Neb Buttress. GR:209 847. 20 minutes.

Neb Buttress is the highest on the edge (15-18m). It is bounded on the right by the obvious Deep Cleft, and is otherwise notable for a pair of imposing aretes – Happy Wanderer and Neb Buttress. The rock is generally good – clean without being polished – but there are some friable flakes.

46.1 Deep Cleft (M) ✳

Dark, deep and private, though less smelly than most of its kind. Climb up the back of the chimney onto a jammed block. Finish outside the capstone with plenty of fresh air and rope drag or by a through route among blocks (no helmets or beer guts).

46.2 Bamford Wall (S) ✳ ✳

Wanders up the slabby wall left of Deep Chimney. Adequate holds and protection await those with eyes to see them. Start up the right-slanting flake near the left edge then get onto a partially detached block. From its right end, step up delicately, trend right, and then left to gain a finger crack and protection. Climb the crack to a big ledge and thread belay. Finish easily or trend left for an exposed finish over shelving holds.

46.3 Happy Wanderer (HVS,5a/b) ✳ ✳

Bold climbing up the central arete. Uncharacteristically protectable. Climb the arete, often using the left wall, to a small overlap below the break. Get as high as possible then reach for a good hold in the break on the left side of the arete

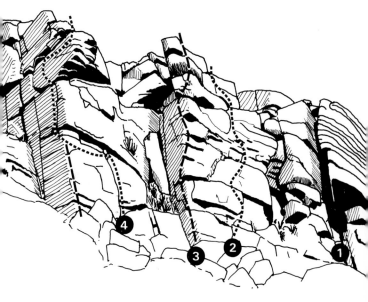

(crux – 5b for short climbers). Get onto the ledge and finish energetically over bulges on the right side of the arete.

46.4 Neb Buttress (HVS,5a) ✳ ✳ ✳

A big route with the crux arriving near the top on slightly overhanging rock. Good protection if you can hang on long enough to place it. Climb a thin crack in the wall right of the arete to the overlap. Traverse left on friable flakes to the arete (or reach this point via the 5a direct start, finishing with a delicate balance move). Move up left to the hand-width crack left of the arete and climb urgently to the break. Move slightly left and climb the wall to another break. Now hand-traverse right as if you mean it and pull onto a shelf.

47: BAMFORD EDGE – GREAT TOR

Summary: Middle-grade crack climbs on a pleasantly situated outcrop.

Crag Conditions: West facing at 400m. Sometimes affected by drainage. Otherwise as for Section 46.

Approach: Initially as for Section 46. Continue for 300m beyond Neb Buttress. Descend below a wrinkled wall to a buttress capped by a large roof. Descend over boulders to the lower tier. GR:207 849. 25 minutes.

Great Tor consists of upper and lower tiers. Gargoyle Flake takes the 12m fluted prow between the wrinkled wall and roofed buttress mentioned in the approach, while the majority of routes take obvious crack lines on the 10-12m lower tier.

47.1 Gargoyle Flake (VS−,4b) ✴ ✴
From the huge block below the prow, layback the flake to good holds and continue to a vegetated ledge. Climb the final nose direct to finish on the gargoyle flutings.

47.2 Sandy Crack (VS−,4b) ✴
Reach over the undercut base of the crack and jam (or otherwise) to an easement. Layback and bridge the wide upper part to an awkward finish.

47.3 Curving Crack (VS,4c) ✴
Semi hand-traverse the easy flake crack leftwards then move up and right on protected undercut jams (or go high with unprotected undercut laybacking) to enter the Sandy Crack easement with a flurry.

47.4 Brown's Crack (VS−,4b) ✴ ✴ ✴
The best route on the Lower Tier, giving clean, varied jamming with good protection. Climb a fingery face crack to a glacis. Jam the slim corner, via one awkward move, to a simple finish.

47.5 Quien Sabe? (VS,4c) ✴ ✴
Start as for Brown's Crack then move left across the glacis, past a flake, to a thin crack in the left arete. Boldly layback the bulge facing left to reach adequate holds and a resting place above. The finish is easy.

47.6 Recess Crack (D+) ✴
The right side of the square-cut recess above a block ledge. Awkward to start.

47.7 Bilberry Crack (VS,5a) ✴ ✴
The protectable finger crack in the left corner of the recess.

47.8 Hasta La Vista (VD) ✴
Climb the left-facing, narrow chimney left of the square-cut recess to a break. Traverse the break rightwards to a crawling exit at the top of the square-cut recess.

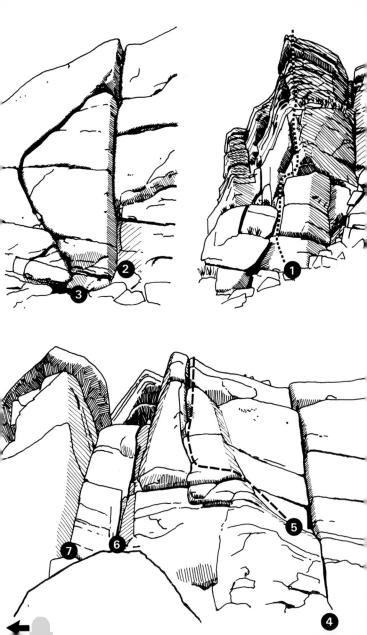

Stanage Edge

Not much needs to be said about Stanage Edge. Without question it contains the greatest number of top-quality routes of all grades on grit. All the ingredients for a gritstone feast are here: perfect rock often set just off-vertical; an average height of 15-20m; a mixture of good lines based on cracks, corners, aretes and buttresses; and a sunny outlook over open, but not bleak, moorland. If it gets more than its fair share of bad weather, then that only serves to make the good days seem that much more special.

The only drawback is that everyone else wants to come to Stanage too. Fortunately there is a solution to this: climb on Black Hawk, Robin Hood and High Neb areas early or late in the day (or midweek or out-of-season), and save Wall End and Stanage End for the peak periods.

Crag Conditions: The edge is set at 425-450m at the crest of Hallam Moors. The main southern part of the edge and High Neb face south-west, whereas Stanage End faces west. Obviously some routes get more or less sun depending on their particular alignment to the crag. The rock is clean, and on bright, breezy days if dries out quickly – even during winter. However, it is exposed to strong winds and is often cloaked in drizzly cloud, while crags set at a slightly lower altitude, such as Froggatt, escape. The rock is sound almost without exception, though highly polished in places on many of the easier classics.

Approach: Refer to the map accompanying the regional introduction to

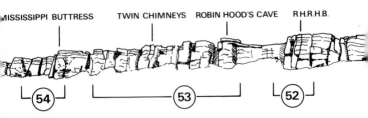

MISSISSIPPI BUTTRESS   TWIN CHIMNEYS   ROBIN HOOD'S CAVE   R.H.R.H.B.

54   53   52

Ladybower and North-East Area (page 121). When travelling from Hathersage on the A625 towards Sheffield, turn left on rising out of the village on the minor Ringinglow road, branching right after a couple of hundred metres. The road rises steeply and after about 2.5km/1.5 miles approaches the right end of the main part of the edge. Turn left here on the Ladybower road. For all areas except High Neb and Stanage End, park on the prepared verge near this junction (GR:244 829). An obvious path leads to the routes in 10-20 minutes. A more direct approach to the Unconquerables and Wall End can be made from the Hollin Bank car park (GR:237 837), 1km/0.5 miles further on. For High Neb and Stanage End, continue along the Ladybower road until about 3km/2 miles from the junction, where there is a parking area at a sharp left-hand bend and cattle grid (GR:227 843). Take the track towards the edge until halfway round a rightwards curve then cross a stile on the left and follow the path up to High Neb (GR:228 853). 20 minutes. For Stanage End (GR:225 866), walk north along the path above the edge for about 20 minutes. Stanage End and High Neb can also be approached from the north via a footpath which leaves the A57 Glossop to Sheffield road at GR:231 878.

Access: Stanage End and High Neb are on private land. Access is allowed (shooting days excepted) provided climbers avoid straying from the rocks. There are no restrictions on the main, southern part of the edge. Dogs should be kept on a lead or left at home.

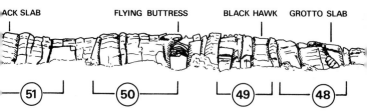

48: STANAGE – GROTTO SLAB AREA

Summary: Corner, wall and buttress routes typical of the high-quality middle-grade climbing at Stanage.

Crag Conditions: Refer to the regional introduction.

Approach: Refer to the regional introduction.

Grotto Slab, a prominent slipped and tilted block, is the most notable feature at the right-hand end of the edge. The slab itself is of only slight interest, though the wall and grooved arete to its left provide two wonderful routes. The two protrusions to the left each contain a good buttress climb. All routes are about 15m in length. Grotto Slab is the most convenient descent, otherwise descend between The Tippler and Flying Buttress.

48.1 Grotto Slab (M) ✳
A useful beginners' route, though awkward rather than interesting. The slanting slab is not as easy as it looks, and there is no protection. Above an optional belay, climb the simple broken wall.

48.2 Heather Wall (S+) ✳✳
An unexpected delight. Climb the wall left of Grotto Slab via horizontal weaknesses; some of the holds are shiny, but they are flat and the moves protectable. The crux arrives just below a ledge at two-thirds height. From the ledge, climb a scoop on the right to an easy finish.

48.3 Crack and Corner (VD+) ✳✳✳
A perfect gritstone route up the grooved arete left of Grotto Slab. Continuously good climbing, with frequent rests and runners. The hardest moves are at the start, where the footholds are badly polished. At two-thirds height, after the main bout of jamming and bridging, move left and climb a flake crack and bulge to a ledge underneath the big overhang. There are good holds over the top for a final, dynamic swing.

48.4 Manchester Buttress (VS–,4c) ✳✳
Start up an off-balance flake crack in the blunt arete then teeter left under the bulge. Move up and traverse awkwardly right to a ledge and an easier finish.

48.5 Gargoyle Buttress (S+) ✳✳
A bigger proposition than Manchester Buttress, though less technical. Start on the right side and finger traverse left above the undercut base of the buttress. Now, watched by the gargoyle peering down from his platform, mantel softly onto a detached block perched on a sloping ledge. Climb the easier wall, shake hands with the gargoyle, then treat yourself to the upper wall on the right.

Crack and Corner (48.3), Stanage

Heather Wall (48.2), Stanage

49: STANAGE – BLACK HAWK AREA

Summary: Polished and popular slits in the lower grades, and a fearsome *E1* above overhangs.

Crag Conditions: Refer to the regional introduction.

Approach: Refer to the regional introduction.

The two corners of the Black Hawk recess each provide a climb, while the other routes make what they can of the intervening wall. Castle Chimney takes the fissure bounding the Tower on its left. The Tippler is the nearest thing to an 'ordinary' route up the undercut buttress further left. Route lengths range from 15-20m. The usual descent is on the left, between The Tippler and Flying Buttress.

49.1 Blizzard Chimney (D) ✳
Start direct or 3m left and enter by a diagonal line. An overhang blocks the exit so step left to finish.

49.2 Black Hawk Hell Crack (S) ✳
Start as for the chimney then climb straight up a steep crack. A hard section near the top has good thread protection.

49.3 Black Hawk Traverse (D+) ✳
Not an ideal beginner's route, though often used as such. Climb a polished break in the centre of the recessed wall to a niche at 5m (runner). Stride left with Henry Bishop then climb a scoop to the easy upper part of Castle Crack.

49.4 Castle Crack (S) ✳ ✳
The ghastly, gleaming corner crack at the left side of the recess. Bold layaways make best use of the initial polished holds.

49.5 Castle Chimney (M) ✳ ✳
Clean, with minimal grovelling. Upper chockstones are passed on the inside by the unimaginative, and on the outside by visionaries.

49.6 The Tippler (E1,5b) ✳ ✳ ✳
A spectacular traverse and baffling crux ensure an unforgettable outing. Protection, thank God, is good. An *in situ* sling usually dangles from a thread at the lip of the top overhang; it can be reached via Tippler Direct (E3,6a), or more realistically by the right edge followed by a finger traverse left across the overhung, undercut wall (a forward-thinking leader will extend runners placed here to avoid rope drag later). Above the lip, a horizontal hand slot left of the thin crack, and a sloping foothold to its right, are the paltry means by which to overcome the crux. The remainder of the crack is a blur.

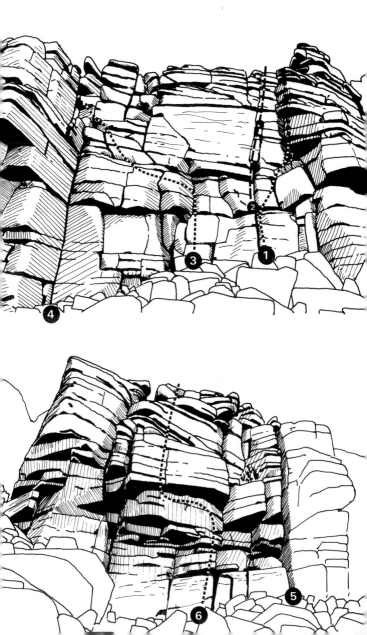

50: STANAGE – FLYING BUTTRESS AREA

Summary: Two of the great gritstone *V.Diffs*.

Approach: Refer to the regional introduction.

Crag Conditions: Refer to the regional introduction.

The 20m normal route on Flying Buttress – climbed direct on heel hooks and adrenalin by Flying Buttress Direct (HVS,5b) – is one of the most popular on the edge. The wall to the left culminates in the 15m corner of Hollybush Crack, a climb of equal quality.

50.1 Flying Buttress (VD) ✳ ✳ ✳
Climb the unprotected lower slab near the left edge (or otherwise) to a ledge. Pull into an undercut groove and climb a flake crack to bulges. Move right high or low and ascend to the terrace. Pull triumphantly over the top overhang.

50.2 Leaning Buttress (VD+) ✳
Climb a block-filled corner to the window at half height, traverse awkwardly left onto the pillar front, then finish up its left edge on rounded holds.

50.3 Hollybush Crack (VD+) ✳ ✳ ✳
Sustained but protectable. Avoid the hard start on the right to gain the first ledge. Enter a niche above (crux) then bridge and layback the upper flake crack.

Flying Buttress (50.1), Stanage

51: STANAGE – BLACK SLAB AREA

Summary: Two of the best *Severe* crack climbs on the edge, plus a poorly-protected *VS* slab. Fingery wall problems provide a diversion.

Crag Conditions: Refer to the regional introduction.

Approach: Refer to the regional introduction.

April Crack and Christmas Crack take the most continuous lines on the face and provide the best climbing at this standard on the edge. To the left the wall angle eases yet further into Black Slab, where Hargreaves's Original Route climbs bravely from crease to crease. The rock to the right of the main section rears up almost to the vertical, losing most of its upright cracks and horizontal creases in the process, to leave the boulderer making the best of it from ruddy excrescences. The major routes are about 15m high, the Rusty Wall climbs about 10m. The most convenient descent is by a tricky scramble to the right of Rusty Wall or, with more difficulty and interest, down Pedestal Chimney on the left of Black Slab. Otherwise descend to the left of Robin Hood's Right-Hand Buttress.

51.1 Rusty Wall Climbs (S+ to VS+,5c) ✳
The crack climbs to left and right can be protected, whereas the two harder climbs on the wall proper are climbed solo – when they are climbed at all. After a fingery start, the central crack of Via Media (VS,4c) proves to be the most normal on the wall. The oppressive left-bounding crack – Green Crack (S+) – is anything but normal, requiring a bold approach and good technique. The wall 2m right of Green Crack – Rugosity Wall (VS+,5c) – eases slightly above a hard start on polished pimples, as does the thin line to the right – Rusty Crack (VS+,5b).

51.2 Right-Hand Trinity (S) ✳
The first notable crack feature on the main face. Climb it direct, bridging the bulge at half height to reach the upper crack.

51.3 Central Trinity (S+) ✳
Disjointed, but includes some good climbing. The break left of Right-Hand Trinity fails to reach the ground so climb a crack on the right for 5m and traverse left to reach its foot. Climb the narrow crack on good holds to the wider and easier upper section.

51.4 Christmas Crack (S) ✳ ✳ ✳
Superb, sustained climbing with good protection up the central face crack. Bridge up the lower groove to gain the crack and climb it ecstatically to the top.

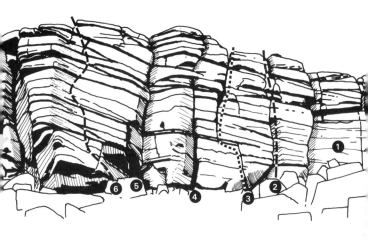

51.5 April Crack (S+) ✳ ✳ ✳

More fine climbing up the perfect shallow groove line to the left of Christmas Crack. Sustained, though nowhere unduly hard, and with good protection. Less polished than you might expect. Enter the crack from the right – tricky – then climb the groove by laying-away and bridging, with one slightly more awkward move near the top.

51.6 Hargreaves's Original Route (VS,4b) ✳ ✳ ✳

Delicate and committing, and with no worthwhile protection, this is no place for an anxiety attack. Start below the right-hand side at an undercut and step awkwardly left onto the middle of the slabby wall. Climb direct, hesitating at a balance move (which can be avoided by a detour to the left edge then back right) to finish near the left edge.

51.7 Pedestal Chimney (D) ✳

The chimney bounding Black Slab on its left is entered via the crack on the left side of its guarding pedestal.

52: STANAGE – ROBIN HOOD'S RIGHT-HAND BUTTRESS

Summary: A high, compact buttress climbed at *Severe* by a notorious wide face crack and at *VS* by a superb groove.

Crag Conditions: Refer to the regional introduction.

Approach: Refer to the regional introduction.

Robin Hood's Right-Hand Buttress consists of a 20m striated wall irregularly undercut at one-third height. The horizontal creases provide the means of transverse or upward progress for all the routes (the crack of the Direct being too wide to be of much use in itself), while the undercuts provide the exposure. Descend with care to the left of the buttress.

52.1 Robin Hood's Right-Hand Buttress Direct (S) ✤ ✤ ✤
An excellent but unnerving climb up the central face crack on the buttress front. Serious. Start at a tight V-groove, climb to the roof, then creep out right to a ledge in the open air. Above rises the feared off-width of the *Buttonhook Crack*, cut at regular intervals by horizontal creases. Because both crack and creases have rounded edges, this upper part used to be the *V.Diff* climber's nightmare – especially when wearing mountain boots and trailing a runnerless rope. Nowadays, despite rock boots and big nuts, it is the *Severe* climber's nightmare. Nevertheless, every move has a secure solution, so take your time and try not to panic.

52.2 Inverted V (VS–,4b) ✤ ✤ ✤
One of the finest VS on grit. Enjoyable, despite some polished footholds, and well-protected throughout. The cracked V-groove at the left side of the buttress front cuts down through the lower band of overhangs to leave a clean, elegant approach of steadily increasing difficulty to The Birdcage beneath the top overhang. Escape by traversing right to finish up a wide crack.

52.3 Ellis's Eliminate (VS,4c) ✤ ✤
Bold, exposed climbing on which the leader must resolve the contradictory desires for progress and protection. Start in the gully left of the buttress and hand-traverse on jams across the twin cracks to the arete. Some re-adjustment to technique will be necessary as the cracks converge. Climb the easing arete in your own time.

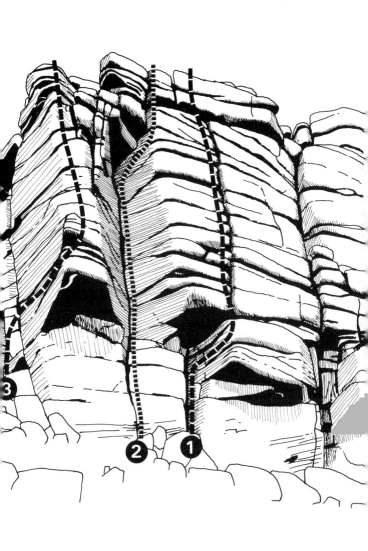

Inverted V (52.2), Stanage

Robin Hood's Right-Hand Buttress Direct (52.1), Stanage

53: STANAGE – ROBIN HOOD'S CAVE AND TWIN CHIMNEYS AREA

Summary: An exhilarating roof finish to a slippery *VS* crack, plus a selection of crack and buttress climbs in the lower grades.

Crag Conditions: Refer to the regional introduction.

Approach: Refer to the regional introduction.

The area comprises a large number of disparate climbs, from the chilling routes entering and leaving Robin Hood's Cave, to the friendlier pitches in and around the Twin Chimneys. Route lengths range from 12-15m. Several descents.

53.1 Robin Hood's Balcony Cave Direct (S) ✳ ✳
Gloomy and difficult with a fortuitous exit. A deeply recessed V-groove leads to the right-hand side of the Balcony Cave; climb it direct, with one detour onto the right wall (polished and difficult), and enter the cave. Finish improbably over the overhang.

53.2 Cave Innominate/Harding's Superdirect Finish (VS+,5a) ✳ ✳
An unsettling, if protectable, route on the left-bounding wall of the buttress. Climb the ragged crackline near the right arete – polished and difficult – to the Balcony Cave (belay). Get out left to the lip of the overhang and overcome it with optimism.

53.3 Right Twin Chimney (D+) ✳
Climb the Right Twin on good layaways up its right-hand rib, stepping into the chimney only for the final few moves. Not difficult, but then not protectable either.

53.4 Left Twin Chimney (D+) ✳ ✳
The more interesting Twin. Can be climbed elegantly by staying on the outside.

53.5 Twin Chimneys Buttress (VS,4c) ✳ ✳
Nice climb, shame about the protection. Climb the arete left of the Twin Chimneys on rounded holds after a hard start on the left side. A delicate step above a block (runner) is the psychological crux.

53.6 Crack and Cave (VD) ✳
Climb the face crack on the left wall of the buttress and enter the cave. Move back onto the block above the crack and traverse the face on the right in a good position to finish pleasantly up shelves.

53.7 Balcony Buttress (VD+) ✳
The broken buttress, heavily striated in its upper part, about 30m left of Twin Chimneys. Start on the right-hand side and trend left when possible to gain the left edge at about half height. Finish direct on rounded holds (exposed).

ROBIN HOOD'S CAVE

TWIN CHIMNEYS

54: STANAGE – MISSISSIPPI BUTTRESS

Summary: Two brilliant routes on the front of a high buttress – a *VS* flake groove and an *HVS* arete – plus a collection of good shorter climbs in the lower grades based on flakes, cracks and chimneys.

Crag Conditions: Refer to the regional introduction.

Approach: Refer to the regional introduction.

Mississippi Buttress has been eaten away at its base, posing a problem for both the Direct, which is trying to reach the flake groove on the right wall, and for Congo Corner, which is intent on climbing the arete. The Chimney on the left side cleaves the undercut and so is unaffected. All three climbs are about 20m long, but each is very different from the others in style and difficulty. The shorter (10m) wall to the left of the buttress provides cameo climbs of equal variety, one of them a contender for the best *V.Diff* on the edge. There is a good descent between wall and buttress.

54.1 Mississippi Buttress Direct (VS–,4b) ✳ ✳ ✳
Possibly the finest route at this grade on the edge. Not as hard as it looks, and well protected. The object is to gain the flake crack in the open groove on the right wall of the buttress; approach steeply via blocks, overcome the bulge at its base with a bold move, then climb it with unbridled joy.

54.2 Congo Corner (HVS,5a) ✳ ✳ ✳
Brilliantly solves the problem of the undercut nose of the buttress. Never easy but stops short of desperation. Protectable. A finger crack in a slender, leaning groove gives a hard start and is best done quickly. Now go left to a good rest ledge. Trend left to a fine flake crack for runners then regain the arete via two creases; either low to gain the ledge with a mantel, or high to gain it with a balance move. You are now irretrievably committed. Ease up on friction and an adequate handhold and grab the fluted spike, your saviour, using it vigorously to gain a ledge above all difficulties.

54.3 Mississippi Chimney (VD) ✳ ✳
The V-chimney on the left side of the buttress fails to reach the ground, leaving a steep and difficult few metres before it can be entered. The chimney proper is more accommodating.

54.4 Heaven Crack (VD) ✳ ✳ ✳
Beautiful climbing (protected semi-laybacking) up the leaning flake on the right side of the wall.

54.5 Hell Crack (VS–,4b) ✳
Less than heavenly climbing up the undercut crack to the left. Overcoming the bulge is the crux. Mind those hands. Protectable.

54.6 Stepladder Crack (S+) ✳
A slight route up cracks to the right of Devil's Chimney. Start up the chimney then move right with difficulty into the thin crack. Climb this and move right into a flake crack for a finish near Hell Crack, or trend left then finish direct.

54.7 Devil's Chimney (VD) ✳ ✳
The genuine article, with some excellent back-and-footing at mid height.

Mississippi Buttress Direct (54.1), Stanage

Left Unconquerable (55.3), Stanage

55: STANAGE – THE UNCONQUERABLES

Summary: Famous laybacks on a vertical face. The unready will be punished.

Crag Conditions: Refer to the regional introduction.

Approach: Refer to the regional introduction.

Nothing subtle about the routes on this 16m buttress: after a common start the Left goes left and the Right goes right. You know what is being asked from the outset. Even the chimney which defines the right-hand side of the face is unequivocal in its demands. Immortalised in the book *Hard Rock,* the Right Unconquerable consequently now looks worse for wear, the perfection of its overlapping flake spoiled by a scar where, during a leader fall, an expanding Friend runner prised off a chunk of the holy grit.

55.1 Curving Chimney (VD) ❋❋
Narrow, clean and unprotected. Climb the first half on the outside, and the second half on the inside. By peeking left at ledges you can get a sneak preview of the following route.

55.2 Right Unconquerable (HVS,5a) ❋❋❋
A formidable undertaking which makes great psychological demands on the leader. Protection is, by necessity, spaced. A jump/reach between the starting crack and a footledge sets the scene. Step right and jam up a little corner, filling it with runners. Then move right and do likewise to the base of the overlapping flake crack. Now go for it, feet high and right to prevent a slip or swing while hands grasp the edge. It seems a long way, but probably isn't, to where you can splay your foot out on a crease for a semi-rest. More of the same, and then suddenly you are tight up against the top overlap and stepping right for another partial rest. There's scope for a hurried scuffle left to finish at the slot, but otherwise it's over the top searching for a barely adequate finger hold to support a leg-flailing finish.

55.3 Left Unconquerable (E1,5b) ❋❋❋
Less strenuous and easier to protect than its superior neighbour, though more technical. After the jump start common to both routes, a sustained bout of semi-laybacking on edges and jams leads to a good hold. The crack now closes, so reach high and get the feet up into a horizontal crease (crux) and, before swivelling off, reach high again into the continuation crack for an easier finish.

56: STANAGE – TOWER FACE AND WALL END

Summary: Three separate buttresses providing a choice of difficult
face, slab or crack climbs, plus a
magnificent *VS* groove.

Crag Conditions: Refer to the
regional introduction.

Approach: Refer to the regional
introduction.

Towards the left end of the main southern section of Stanage, the edge begins
to break up into isolated buttresses separated by short walls or broken rock –
though the buttresses themselves lack nothing in stature or quality. Most
routes are 16-20m long, while Tower Face is about 25m. There are several easy
descents between the buttresses.

56.1 Tower Face (VS+,5a) ✳ ✳
The main difficulties are concentrated in the sketchily protected lower half.
Gain a friable flake in the wall left of the right-bounding chimney with difficulty
and use it to reach the horizontal break. Move left and climb the more
substantial flake to finish.

56.2 Goliath's Groove (VS+,5a) ✳ ✳ ✳
A superb climb in two distinct parts – an off-width cracked groove, and a thin
corner crack. Bridge the smooth walls of the unprotected lower groove until
the crack narrows sufficiently for jams and runners. From the midway ledge,
semi-layback the protectable upper crack to the top.

56.3 Wall End Crack (S) ✳ ✳
A fine, underrated crack climb on the face left of the Goliath's Groove buttress.
Jam the difficult initial crack to a ledge then avoid the wide crack above by
climbing the slabby face to its left. The continuation is initially of chimney width
but soon narrows to a good finishing crack.

56.4 Wall End Slab (VS–,5b) ✳
The start is unduly hard and the easier (4a/b), escapable upper section poorly
protected. A block supports the main bulk of the slab; climb this with difficulty
near its left side to a ledge. Continue up the slab almost to a sloping shelf
(runner) then traverse right on creases to finish near the right edge.

56.5 Fern Crack (VS,4c) ✳ ✳
Classic crack climbing with no surprises. Climb the initial leaning crack to a
ledge, move up to enter the main crack, and climb it finishing left.

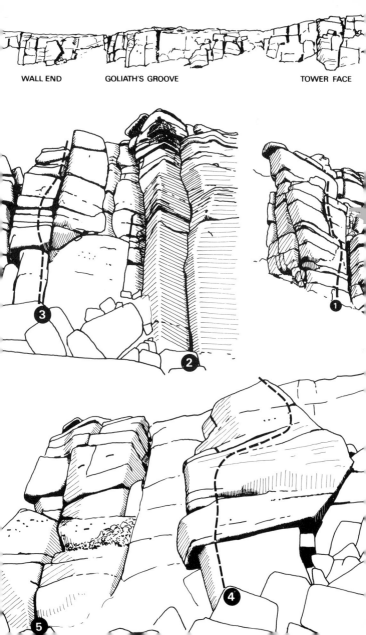

WALL END   GOLIATH'S GROOVE   TOWER FACE

57: STANAGE – HIGH NEB

Summary: Good, if not great, climbs on a slightly less popular part of the edge, representing a wide variety of styles and difficulties.

Crag Conditions: Refer to the regional introduction.

Approach: Refer to the regional introduction (note the access restriction).

The High Neb area is the main attraction at the north end of the Stanage escarpment. It consists of a continuous outcrop shaped by the usual mix of aretes, cracks, corners and overhangs. High Neb Buttress climbs the slabby face of the tower near the right-hand end of the group, while Inaccessible Crack takes the left corner of the recess left of the most prominent roof (climbed at E2,5c by Quietus). Route lengths are around 15m. Descend easily to left or right, or down the gully (M) left of High Neb Buttress.

57.1 Eric's Eliminate (S) ✳
The roof of Kelly's Overhang (HVS,5b) puts a twist in Twisting Crack (S), but this face crack to its left is far more pleasant to climb. The start and finish of the crack are jammed, whereas the middle section is best climbed using wall holds. Good protection throughout.

57.2 Inaccessible Crack (VS,4c) ✳ ✳
Disjointed but finds some good, well-protected moves (double ropes will help protect the second on the initial crack). The hanging corner crack at the left side of the recess can be reached direct with relative ease. However, the usual indirect approach climbs a thin crack in the middle of the recessed wall – hard to start and finish – then traverses across a break line into the corner. The corner itself is less difficult than it appears. (Impossible Slab (E2,5c) climbs the wall and slab between the start of Inaccessible Crack and Eckhard's Chimney (VD), the right-bounding corner of the recess.)

57.3 Norse Corner Climb (S+) ✳ ✳
A bit of a rogue, but a good route if you can get up the first few moves. Start beneath the big roof, gain the inset slab by a hard pocket move (4c), then climb the ramp on the right – still difficult but protectable (alternatively, gain the ramp by a polished layback). From the small ledge at the end of the ramp, which could have been reached by a cop-out entry from the right, use better holds to get up left onto the big ledge. Layback the corner crack to easier ground.

57.4 Tango Crack (VD) ✳
Climb directly up the easing crack in the wall left of High Neb Buttress.

57.5 High Neb Buttress (VS+,4c) ❈ ❈ ❈

A serious and delicate face climb with useful protection only at half height. Start just right of the cutaway and make a series of balance moves up the face, easing slightly, towards a horizontal break and protection for the crucial mantel onto the break itself. The next section, though still delicate, gradually eases to a simple finish.

Inaccessible Crack (57.2), Stanage

58: STANAGE – STANAGE END

Summary: Serious slab climbs on a secluded face.

Crag Conditions: Refer to the regional introduction.

Approach: Refer to the regional introduction (note the access restriction).

The climbs wander over the featureless rough rock of the 12m slipped block, or the face to its right.

58.1 The Pinion (VD+) ✳

Start near the left edge and trend right via a pocket move (crux, unprotected) to a small ledge two-thirds way up the slab. Traverse the break left and finish up the arete.

58.2 The Ariel (VD+) ✳

Start at the rib left of the cutaway and trend delicately left, mantelling onto the Pinion ledge (crux). Finish trending right.

58.3 The Green Streak (VS,4b) ✳

Start as for Ariel then climb the slab trending slightly right.

58.4 Prospero's Climb (VD) ✳ ✳

Protectable and the best introduction to Stanage End. Climb a flake crack then move left at a break and mantel onto it (crux). Layback the second flake crack and step left to a ledge.

58.5 The Crab Crawl (S) ✳

Ascend the poorly-protected face between Prospero's and the arete, trending slightly right.

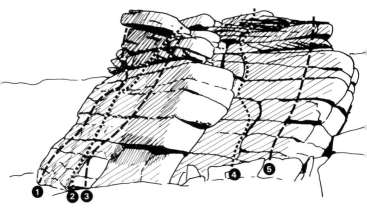

Burbage Moor

(Refer to the map accompanying the regional introduction to Ladybower and North-East Area on page 121.)

Burbage Moor lies adjacent to Stanage, sharing much of its moorland outlook, if little of its climbing character. In this respect the region is one of great contrasts, from the gloomy, forbidding buttresses of the South Edge, to the sunny, inviting craglets of the North Edge.

Burbage North Edge is the Windgather of the north-east: lots of little climbs, the best of which are often in the lower grades. True, you have to work a little harder on the spaced holds of this more rounded rock, and the very best climbing creeps into the *Severe* and *VS* categories, though in return the routes have more individual character. It is paradise for the competent solo climber.

Two sections of the North Edge rise above the ordinary – Hollyash Wall and the Amazon area. Some of the climbing elsewhere on the edge is equally as good, but the added lengths of these routes helps fix them in memory. The best on Hollyash Wall is The Knight's Move, though at *VS* this may be harder than most people climbing here will want to attempt. Of several good climbs in the Amazon area, Amazon Crack itself is the perfect *Hard Severe* jam crack.

Ignoring the quarries of Burbage South, the most imposing of the natural buttresses – The Keep – provides the two selected routes. Brooks's Crack and Byne's Crack are both outstanding climbs at the upper and lower limits of the *VS* grade.

Higgar Tor is renowned for its strenuous hard routes on the overhanging face of the Leaning Block. The Rasp is the classic of the face but too hard for this selection. Enjoy instead the gentle caress of The File on the merely vertical end face.

Access: There are no restrictions on access to these crags. Dogs should be kept on a lead or, better still, left at home.

The Knight's Move (59.7), Burbage

59: BURBAGE NORTH – SENTINEL AREA AND HOLLYASH WALL

Summary: Short face and crack climbs on a friendly moorland crag.

Crag Conditions: South-west facing at 400m. Prone to bad weather, but idyllic on fine evenings. Dries quickly on sunny or breezy days. Very popular during summer weekends.

Approach: (i) Northern approach. From the A625 Hathersage to Sheffield road, turn north 1.5km/1 mile from Hathersage towards Ringinglow. Roadside parking after 4km/2.5 miles, shortly after crossing Upper Burbage Bridge (GR:263 829). Follow the Green Drive south until Hollyash Wall can be identifiled on the left. GR:268 822. 15 minutes.

(ii) Southern approach. From Hathersage follow the A625 towards Sheffield and park soon after a tight right bend at Burbage Bridge (GR:263 806). Follow the Green Drive north until the Hollyash Wall can be identified on the right. GR:268 822. 25 minutes.

Burbage North gains height near its southern end to provide the slightly longer (10-14m) Hollyash Wall climbs. To their left, a cluster of miniature climbs (8-9m) near the prow of The Sentinel (E2,5c) increase options in the lower grades.

59.1 Black Slab (S+) ✲
The left edge of the slabby face left of the twin prows.

59.2 Black Slab Variation (D+) ✲
The indefinite crack and scoop to the right of Black Slab.

59.3 Sentinel Chimney (D+) ✲
The protectable V-chimney between the prows.

59.4 Sentinel Crack (D) ✲
Semi-layback the crack right of The Sentinel to a large ledge then layback a wide corner crack above.

59.5 Green Crack (VD) ✲
Better than it looks (or sounds). Climb the left-hand, block-filled wide crack.

59.6 Hollyash Crack (VS–,4b) ✲
Easy at first then knee-jam a smooth crack to reach better holds. Trend right to finish.

59.7 The Knight's Move (VS,4c) ✲✲
Gain the left end of the overhang (runner) and layback the shallow flake crack. Move up past a horizontal break to a wider break and finish trending right.

59.8 The Big Chimney (S) ✲
Impressive. A knee jam may help overcome the undercut base. Bridge right below the capstone onto a small ledge for a straightforward finish.

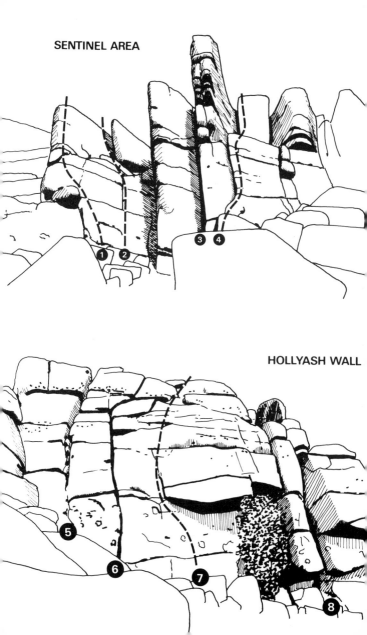

SENTINEL AREA

HOLLYASH WALL

60: BURBAGE NORTH – AMAZON AREA

Summary: Perfect miniature corner and crack climbs.

Crag Conditions: As for Section 59.

Approach: Refer to Section 59. The Amazon area lies a few hundred metres south of Hollyash Wall, near the right-hand end of the North Edge.

Here the edge again reaches sufficient height to warrant rope protection (8-10m). The rock is rough but not brutal.

60.1 Brooks's Layback (S+) ✳✳
A perfect little corner crack tucked out of sight at the left end of this group. Ignore Brooks's advice and jam blissfully to the top.

60.2 Wobblestone Crack (VD+) ✳
The undercut start on polished, rounded holds is crucial. The wobbly block does.

60.3 Amazon Crack (S+) ✳✳✳
A magnificent jam crack up a slender corner. Not as hard as it looks, and well protected.

60.4 Long Tall Sally (E1,5c) ✳✳
The sketchily protected fingertip crack in the shallow corner at the left side of the recess.

60.5 Greeny Crack (VS−,4b) ✳
The wide crack in the right-hand corner of the recess

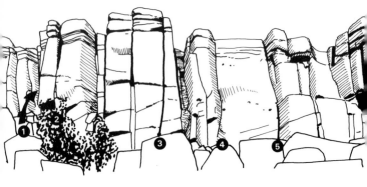

Greeny Crack (60.4), Burbage

61: BURBAGE SOUTH – THE KEEP

Summary: Twin *VS* crack climbs, at the lower and upper limits of the grade, on an impending, gloomy buttress.

Crag Conditions: North-west facing at 400m and therefore often cold and damp from late autumn to early spring. The crag top is clean, but both cracks seep drainage for a while after wet weather. Much less popular than the North Edge.

Approach: From Hathersage follow the A625 towards Sheffield and park soon after a tight right bend at Burbage Bridge (GR:263 806). Cross the stile at the start of the Green Drive then bear right immediately and follow a path over the bracken covered shoulder above Burbage Quarry to a pile of boulders 30m from the top of the South Edge (the path is still rising gently here). The buttress below is The Keep. GR:268 813. 15 minutes. Alternatively, walk along the Green Drive from either end and approach the buttress from below over bracken and heather.

Like the North Edge, the natural grit of the South Edge is rough and solid. But on the higher buttresses an atmosphere of seriousness pervades, due only in part to the lack of sunshine until late afternoon. The good routes are harder, and the general outlook less friendly. At 14m The Keep is highest of the natural Burbage buttresses, and its two crack climbs the most compelling at this standard. The awesome face to the left of Brooks's is climbed by the incredible Partheon Shot (XS,7a).

61.1 Brooks's Crack (VS+,5a) ✳ ✳ ✳
The left-hand crack, complicated by bulges and of steadily increasing difficulty. Good protection (some large nuts required), but still a big undertaking. Avoid green, oozing stuff in the tapering corner by climbing the wall, then step right at its top and pull into the first niche. Reach over the bulge to enter the second niche. Another bulge guards entry to the final hand/fist crack, which is dealt with by udging or an asset-splitting exercise in wide bridging.

61.2 Byne's Crack (VS–,4b) ✳ ✳ ✳
A more pleasant way of covering essentially the same ground. Start by jamming a perfect crack, pausing for thought only at the exit. Climb a short chimney then get high on undercuts and layback into the finishing crack on the right.

62: HIGGAR TOR – THE FILE

Summary: The magnificent hand-mauling jamming crack up the end wall of the famous Leaning Block. Easily accessible and a must for all masochistic grit fanciers on a flying visit.

Crag Conditions: South-east facing at 400m. Clean and takes no drainage so dries quickly. This is a popular tourist spot, though the unhelpful angle of the rock limits interest from climbers.

Approach: From the A625 Hathersage to Sheffield road, turn north 1.5km/1 mile from Hathersage on the minor Ringinglow road. After about 1.5km/1 mile, the overhanging face of the Leaning Block will be seen directly ahead. Continue past left and right bends and park on the verge before reaching the road junction (GR:256 823). Cross the step stile opposite onto the path leading to the crag top, but then fork right on a contouring path to gain the foot of the Leaning Block (GR:256 818). 5 minutes.

The Leaning Block of Higgar Tor is a unique gritstone feature, overhanging by 4m in a height of 12m. The names of the original routes reveal something of what to expect from the rock: Surform (HVS,5a), which climbs flakes on the left side of the face then finishes left again; and The Rasp (E2,5b), which starts up the flakes and continues up their right-trending line. By comparison, the route on the merely vertical end face is a jaunt. Descent from the summit of the block is by a reverse mantel and a step down from the north-east corner.

62.1 The File (VS+,4c) ✳ ✳ ✳
A sustained pitch to delight the proficient jammer. Others will be cowed and emerge, if at all, exhausted. Excellent protection available from large nuts. Climb the main crack, passing a small overhang low down, to a good hold at its top. A hand-rasping transfer left leads to the final crack and secure exit holds.

Millstone and Lawrencefield Quarries

(Refer to the map accompanying the regional introduction to Ladybower and North-East Area on page 121.)

Among such wealth of natural grit the notion of climbing up the ragged cracks and poised blocks of a quarry seems crazy. And it would be if the routes weren't so good. The technical intricacy of the thin face cracks, walls and corners of Millstone Edge and, only to a slightly lesser extent, Lawrencefield, overcome all prejudices against the medium. It helps that these are no dismal quarried holes, but a string of sunny bays, each with their own character.

Both quarries received a bashing from the peg merchants in the 1950s and 1960s. We have them to thank for the existence of many of the routes. The finger cracks of the Embankment simply could not be climbed at a reasonable standard but for the repeated insertion and removal of progressively fatter pegs. Put your moral sensibilities on one side and enjoy the climbing.

Many of the great Millstone routes are too hard for this selection, but by bending the self-imposed top limit to include a few *E1*s on the Embankment, it will serve as an introduction.

Not all the routes are hard: Brixton Road and The Scoop share the big feel of the crag at *V.Diff* and less. There's also a handful of good *VS* routes, though to sample the crag's true potential you need to be climbing at *HVS*. Some of the routes at this grade are among the best on grit. Great Portland Street, Bond Street and Great North Road are magnificent. At *E1* you can set off on the Embankment's unremitting finger cracks – Route 4 and Time For Tea Original – and glimpse something of the style of the big routes without suffering their accompanying verticality and lack of protection.

Some of the Millstone quality transfers across the road to Lawrencefield. Here some of the best lines are in the lower and medium grades; *V.Diffs* don't come much more exciting than Pulpit Route, or *VS*s more absorbing than Great Harry.

Access: There are no restrictions on access. Dogs should be kept on a lead or, better still, left at home.

The Mall Area (64), Millstone

63: MILLSTONE – KEYHOLE CAVE AREA

Summary: Intimidating quarry climbing in the lower and middle grades.

Crag Conditions: Generally west facing at 325m, though some routes remain shaded by adjacent north-facing walls (a blessing on hot summer days). The walls are topped by shattered layers of rock, so after rain some holds may be covered in grit. The edge is exposed to strong westerlies. Very popular during summer evenings and weekends, when there is a real risk of stonefall. Rock belay anchors at the top are generally poor so it is usual to supplement these with one or more fence posts (this consumes a lot of rope). The corner start of Skywalk is slow to dry and is difficult when greasy.

Approach: Via the A625 Hathersage to Sheffield road. Limited layby parking about 3km/2 miles from Hathersage, just before the road bends sharp left at the Surprise View (GR:248 801). If this is full there is a large car park a few hundred metres further on towards Sheffield. A track leads left below the quarry, and from which separate paths lead into the individual bays. The first bay is uninspiring, the second includes a wall cut by the distinctive Keyhole Cave. GR:248 804. 5 minutes.

The main wall of the bay contains two shallow caves at half height: the Keyhole Cave on the left and an unnamed cave on the right. Gimcrack climbs the cracked and grooved wall left of the lesser cave, while Skywalk starts up the corner left of the Keyhole Cave then finishes on the exposed wall above its roof. Brixton Road finds a way up the cracked and less steep wall to the left. Route lengths are 20-25m. Descend with care over ledges in the corner at the right-hand end of the wall.

63.1 Gimcrack (VS,4c) ✳ ✳

Not a compelling line, but a useful introduction to Millstone climbing. Adequate protection. On the wall between the two caves is a wide crack – Shaftesbury Avenue (HVS,5a). Start to the right of this and climb a crack until it is possible to move left, past another crack, into the base of the shallow corner (all very steep). Climb the corner then move right above a small overhang and finish direct with trepidation over ball-bearing ledges.

63.2 Skywalk (VS–,4b) ✳ ✳

A gloomy start contrasts with an exposed finish above the Keyhole Cave. Not technically hard but difficult to protect. Bridge and jam the corner then exit awkwardly onto the first of the big ledges. Ignore a grotty direct finish and, from a belay on the uppermost ledge, creep round the arete into the blasting exposure of the headwall above the Keyhole Cave. Climb diagonally right on suspect face holds, unprotected and only just in balance, to a thin crack

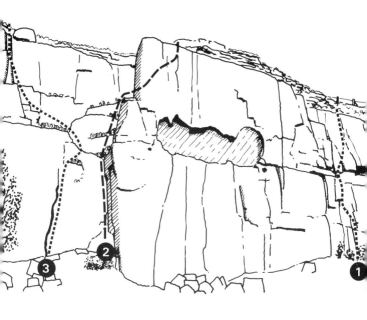

(runner). Ignore this possible exit and continue trending right to an easier, but still gritty, finish. Belay anchors well back as usual.

63.3 Brixton Road (VD) ❋ ❋

Climbs a big face with surprising ease, though flawed by the break at mid height. Protectable. Start up the wide face crack and climb it with interest trending right. Trend right then left up ledges (possibly belay) to a long ledge, which is traversed left almost to its end. Make a rising traverse left on ledges to enter a slim corner and climb this for a few metres until a crack in the left wall leads to an open finish on the left arete. Care required on gritty shelves at the top. Fence belays.

64: MILLSTONE – THE MALL AREA

Summary: Three great climbs –
a corner, a shallow groove and a face
crack – on top-quality quarried grit.
The exposed arete of Covent Garden
provides a contrast in position and
technique.

Crag Conditions: Refer to Section 63 for general comments. The
corner of The Mall, and to some extent Great Portland Street, remain
shaded by London Wall until late in
the afternoon.

Approach: As for Section 63. The
corner of The Mall is a prominent
feature in the huge bay left of the
Keyhole Cave area.

London Wall (E5,6a), a famous Millstone testpiece, ascends the vertical and
peg-scarred right wall of the big corner of The Mall. Wider cracks and grooves
cut the broader and off-vertical left wall. The first of these is the slim groove of
Great Portland Street, while the jam crack to its left is taken by Bond Street.
Covent Garden finds a way up the more broken wall to its left before finishing
up the sharp left arete. Route lengths range from 20-30m. The usual descent
is by broken rocks at the far left end of the bay.

64.1 The Mall (VS+,4c) ✳ ✳
The big corner, gritty and sustained. Frequently underestimated. Protection is
less good than you might think. In several places the corner crack opens to
fist/foot width, though a crack in the right wall helps.

64.2 Great Portland Street (HVS,5b) ✳ ✳ ✳
A superb route up the slim, bottomless groove. High in the grade. The groove
is compact and so protection is spaced, particularly for the main bridging
sequence at half height. Enter the initial groove by a hard semi-mantel – the
technical crux – and bridge it with echoes of Tremadog's Wasp and First Slip
to good finger jams and runners in the corner crack. The groove steepens but
there is now better protection for some wide bridging on spaced holds to an
exit left onto a ledge. Continue over ledgy but compact rock to large ledges
just below the top. Belays well back.

64.3 Bond Street (HVS,5a) ✳ ✳ ✳
A wonderful jamming pitch, narrowing from wide-hand to finger width, up the
steepening face crack. Sustained but well protected. Low in the grade. Enter
the crack and jam up it to enter the pod. Continue by the narrower crack and
layback into a niche. Exit by finger jams (crux) to better holds. Step left to a
ledge with belay anchors in the overhung corner above. Finish easily to left or
right, or by the arete pitch of Covent Garden.

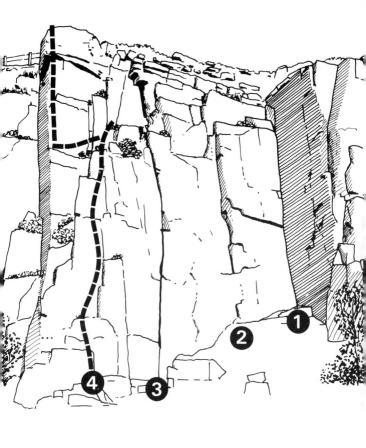

64.4 Covent Garden (VS,4b) ✳✳

A mediocre start, but a fine exposed finish on a sharp arete. The arete is not hard but is difficult to protect. Start between the left arete and a small corner on the right, and find the easiest way up the wall to the big break at half height (belay anchors up on the right in an overhung corner). Descend a little and traverse a shelf to the left arete. Climb the right side of the exposed arete to a ledge (possible runners). Continue by similar means to the top. The finish is cleaner than usual, though not entirely sound. Belay anchors well back.

65: MILLSTONE – EMBANKMENT WALL

Summary: Fingery climbing up off-vertical, peg-scarred face cracks. Addictive.

Crag Conditions: As for Section 63. Depending on the season, the routes nearest the corner may remain shaded until late afternoon – a plus point on warm days.

Approach: As for Section 63. The Embankment Wall is situated just left of The Mall area in the huge bay beyond that of the Keyhole Cave.

The Embankment Wall used to be a peggers' playground, and we have them to thank – or blame – for the series of clean finger cracks that now score the wall. There are few face holds to supplement the toe jams and layaways, which are rapidly becoming polished. Protection is good, but trying to place it all will sap strength and upset rhythm. The wall is highest (30m) near the corner of Whitehall (HVS,5a) at its right-hand side, climbed here by the merging twin cracks of Route 4 and Time For Tea Original. Route 3 is equally sustained, though there is less of it (20m). The slightly shorter Route 2 is of quite different character, consisting of an over-wide jamming crack. The routes finish on a broken terrace, on which belay anchors are sometimes less reliable than is suggested by their evident regular use, so back-ups are wise. Optional finishes are available on the friable upper wall, though the usual way off is to scramble up the terrace (care with loose rocks) then descend the break at the far left end of the bay.

65.1 Embankment Route 4 (E1,5b) ✳ ✳ ✳
Relentless, fingery climbing up the right-hand crack. Climb the first section, inevitably straying into the Whitehall corner, then overcome a sustained stretch to a Thank God hold at the base of a slim groove. Climb the groove on layaways and pinches then move onto a foot ledge on the right. Reach for the sloping top ledge and step left to finish.

65.2 Time for Tea Original (E1,5b) ✳ ✳ ✳
A more sustained version of Route 4. Climb the crack 1m left of the Route 4 start – none of it easy – to its top (a hard finish goes out left here). Make a long stride right into Route 4 and move up to the Thank God hold at the base of the slim groove. Finish as for Route 4.

65.3 Embankment Route 3 (E1,5b) ✳ ✳
Another hard face crack (they get more familiar but no easier). At first the crack is generally wider than that on Route 4, with more footholds and pinches, plus a few poor hand jams. Where the crack thins and slants left, reach to face holds on the right. When stood on these, success is assured.

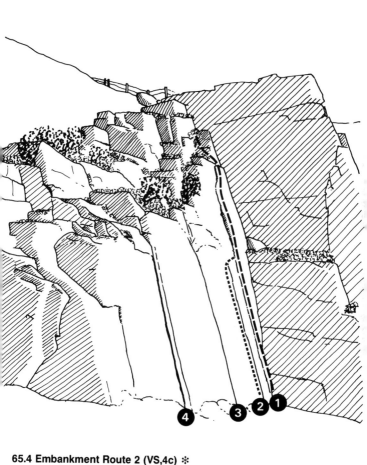

65.4 Embankment Route 2 (VS,4c) ✳

An unhelpful wide crack on the left side of the wall. Those attempting it by pure layback are doomed to fail. Climb the left-hand and wider of twin cracks by a mixture of painful laybacks and jams, using the right-hand crack for protection if you've left the big guns behind.

66: MILLSTONE – GREAT NORTH ROAD

Summary: One of the most satisfying routes of this grade on quarried
grit. The Scoop shares some of its atmosphere at a low level of technical
difficulty.

Crag Conditions: As for Section

63. Great North Road remains
shaded until later in the day.

Approach: As for Section 63. The
routes are just left of the Embankment Wall in the huge bay left of that
of the Keyhole Cave.

A large recess left of the Embankment Wall tapers to a final hanging corner –
the spectacular finish to Great North Road. To its left are the sharply defined
corners and aretes which in turn have represented the ultimate in difficulty and
seriousness at Millstone: Great West Road (E1,5b), the slim left-hand groove
and upper arete; Green Death (E4,5c), the compact open corner; Edge Lane
(E5,5c), the left arete of Green Death; and Master's Edge (E7,6c), effectively the
direct start of Great Arete (E5,5c) which climbs the upper right arete of Green
Death. Among all this desperation The Scoop adventures upwards on ledges
and large holds. The quarry is at its highest here and route lengths attain 35m.
Descend by the break at the far left end of the bay.

66.1 Great North Road (HVS,5a) ✳ ✳ ✳
A superb corner line – complicated by ramps, ledges and overhangs – with
a terrific atmosphere. Protection is good when it matters, as is rock quality.
Where the starting crack veers left, climb steeply up to the right to a ledge
below the corner proper. A smooth corner layback (crux) leads to an isolated
ledge. The corner above is capped by an overhang but face holds
miraculously appear on the left wall. At the overhang, move left in a position of
extreme exposure and climb the final hanging corner.

66.2 The Scoop (D+) ✳ ✳
The best of the easier routes at Millstone. Not always easy to protect so
requires a confident leader. The cone of slab left of Great North Road is split
on its left side by a crack; climb it easily to steeper rock then ascend a groove,
and its left wall, to ledges at half height. Climb the first of the upper corners by
a shattered-looking but reasonably sound break on its right wall, and avoid the
second by a (genuinely) shattered break to its right.

Great North Road (66.1), Millstone

Great Slab (67.1), Millstone

67: MILLSTONE – GREAT SLAB

Summary: A smooth slab topped by steeper rock more typical of quarry climbing.

Crag Conditions: As for Section 63. The slab is green with lichen, though when dry the loss of friction is due to polished holds.

Approach: As for Section 63. Follow the path leftwards below the quarry to a bay dominated by a large trapezoid slab.

The slabby angle is unique at Millstone, and rare on any quarried grit. Most of it is hopelessly smooth, but towards the right side it is split by a thin crack to give a starting point for Great Slab. A shallow corner bounding the left side of the slab provides the layback holds for Svelt. Great Slab is about 25m high, Svelt about 20m. Descend left of the left adjoining bay, or right of the right adjoining bay (as for Great North Road etc.).

67.1 Great Slab (VS,4c) ✵✵
Thin slab climbing contrasts with a more conventional finish. Not much protection on the slab. Climb the thin crack right of centre by energetic finger layaways and foot friction (or work the feet up the crack – equally precarious). A runner protects the transfer to an easier crack on the right which leads to the top of the slab. Climb a wide crack to a square-cut ledge below the headwall. Finish by climbing a shallow recess in the shattered band, with an awkward move below the top.

67.2 Svelt (VS+,4c) ✵✵
Another disjointed climb, though again successfully mixes delicate slab work with a strenuous finish. Better protection on the slab section than the previous route. Climb the slanting corner at the left end of the slab and exit via a large slanting hold on the left. The original finish (at least HVS,5a) moves right to climb a trying and increasingly difficult shallow groove tufted with grass. However, to maintain the standard move left from the slab exit and climb a short, overhanging, corner crack (good protection) by a hurried layback and reachy finish. Finish easily up the large recess.

68: LAWRENCEFIELD – POOL AREA (Left)

Summary: A classic *VS* and two good easier climbs in a pleasantly secluded quarry.

Crag Conditions: As for Section 69. These routes all ascend a south facing wall.

Approach: As for Section 69.

The pool is contained on its left side by a smooth wall and arete, to the left of which is the big corner of Great Harry. Pulpit Route climbs a slanting line to the left of this corner before crossing it near the top, while Three Tree Climb takes a discontinuous line up cracks and grooves further left. Route lengths range from 20-25m. Top belay anchors are scarce, so when possible it is wise to take a stance just below the top, thereby freeing sufficient rope to reach distant anchors or to link several of the poor fence posts. Descend to the left.

68.1 Three Tree Climb (S) ✲ ✲
Pleasant groove climbing with a gymnastic start and an optional hard finish. Good protection. Gain the pillar top from the right via a semi-mantel on a flake ledge (or alternatively from the left). Ascend the groove above until forced by its compact continuation into the hanging flake groove on the right (there's something useful hidden around the right arete). Continue to a tree belay (back-ups advisable). Step left to a ledge and finish up short corners, or, from a higher ledge on the right, climb a cracked wall and step left just below the top (S+ but protectable).

68.2 Pulpit Route (VD) ✲ ✲
Technically reasonable after the awkward start, but with a serious feel. Avoid if damp or gritty. Protection is merely adequate. Start up a hard crack and use wall holds on the left to gain ledges. Follow the ramp up to the right and climb a wide corner crack to the Pulpit belay. Stride across the gap on the right to a ledge and follow an exposed ramp to a region of ledges on the right. Finish up the back corner.

68.3 Great Harry (VS+,4c) ✲ ✲ ✲
Unremitting but well protected. Bridge and jam the corner past a halfway rest to the Pulpit. Climb the wide and gently overhanging corner crack above and step left to a ledge below the final corner (belay advisable). Bridge the corner to a gritty finish.

69: LAWRENCEFIELD – POOL AREA (Right)

Summary: A wandering approach to a superbly positioned *VS* layback crack, plus a selection of short climbs on a subsidiary wall.

Crag Conditions: The generally west-facing quarry is situated at 275m in a more sheltered location than Millstone. Birch trees and a pool below the crag add to the charm (though not the beer cans floating on the water). However, it is best avoided when the midges are active. Quieter and less austere than Millstone. The approach to Excalibur could be complicated by high water levels.

Approach: Via the A625 Hathersage to Sheffield road. Park in a layby about 3km/2 miles from Hathersage, just before the road bends sharp left at the Surprise View (GR:248 801). If this is full there is a large car park a few hundred metres further on towards Sheffield. Cross a wall near a tottering buttress on the outside of the bend and follow a path past two inferior bays to the pool area. 5 minutes.

The formidable headwall behind the pool provides only *Extreme* climbing, except at its upper right end where the shallow cracked corner of Excalibur awaits. This corner is approached by traversing ledges above the pool and climbing a narrow, subsidiary wall (total route length, 30m). The other routes climb the 10m high wedge of compact slabby rock – Gingerbread Slab – to the right of the pool. Belay anchors are better than usual above this face. It is worth setting up an abseil if intending to climb several of the Gingerbread routes (use a sling and krab to avoid harming the tree). Otherwise ascend broken ground to the top and descend to the left as usual.

69.1 Excalibur (VS,4c) ✳ ✳
The corner asserts itself only in the top 7m, but it's worth waiting for. Traverse ledges above the right-hand side of the pool to the large shelf. The lower corner is vegetated so climb the giant's staircase on the right to a ledge. There are no convenient belay anchors here so it is best to continue (a 45m rope will just reach from the shelf to the tree belay at the top). Step left to sudden exposure and good runners in the corner, then climb it by bridging and a final, frantic layback on a good edge. There are monster finishing holds for the exit to a ledge just below the top. This is the best stance, but it's worth first tying-off a tree well back from the edge as a back-up anchor.

69.2 Limpopo Groove (VS–,4b) ✳
Ascend the corner left of the slabby wall by bridging and face climbing to a hard finish. Well protected.

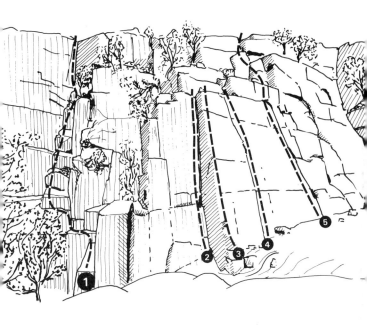

69.3 Gingerbread (VS−,4b) ✻✻

Climb the unprotected (but reversible) left edge of the slabby wall to a narrow ledge at half height. Mediocre runners protect a delicate step up (crux) at two-thirds height. The final few moves ought to feel easier but don't.

69.4 Merinque (VS+,4c) ✻

A thinner and even less protected version of Gingerbread up the vague crack line 3m right of the arete. After a delicate start, better holds lead to the halfway point and some poor protection for a delicate step-up a little higher.

69.5 Snail Crack (VD) ✻

The simplest and safest route to the ledge. Don't climb the obvious system of breaks but a slim crack to the left (crux at two-thirds height). Mantel onto the big ledge to finish. Climb over ledges and short walls to the top.

Froggatt/Curbar Escarpment

Froggatt and Curbar edges are part of near-continuous escarpment above the eastern rim of the Derwent Valley. Set at a lower altitude than the moorland edges further north, they are part of a more pastoral scene. Village noises drift up from below; woodland extends to the base of the rocks; and the pubs are within strolling distance of the crags.

Some say Froggatt rock, rough without being malicious, is the best on grit. It obeys no uniform angle or characteristic set of features, so if you like grit slabs best (or jamming cracks, or pinnacles, or overhangs, or chimneys, or corners), then you will surely find something here to confirm your good taste. Some of the faces have been quarried, but so long ago that they have weathered back into a neo-natural state, their sordid history politely overlooked.

The big slab routes at Froggatt escape inclusion by at least a couple of grades; the smaller Sunset Slab and Three Pebble Slab must suffice. Heather Wall and Hawk's Nest Crack are popular among the hand-jammers, while fans of Swimmer's Chimney or Tody's Wall are, it's true, harder to come by. Froggatt Pinnacle is the dominant feature of the edge, and Valkyrie a contender for the best route on gritstone.

In a geographical sense, Curbar is merely a southern extension to Froggatt. From a rock climber's point of view it is quite different. The effects of quarrying are more evident, and more consequential. The best routes are, on average, a grade harder than at Froggatt; so although PMC1 and Bel Ami at *Mild VS* are good, The Peapod and Maupassant at solid *HVS* are better.

Access: There are no restrictions on access when approaching the crags as described. Dogs should be kept on a lead or, better still, left at home.

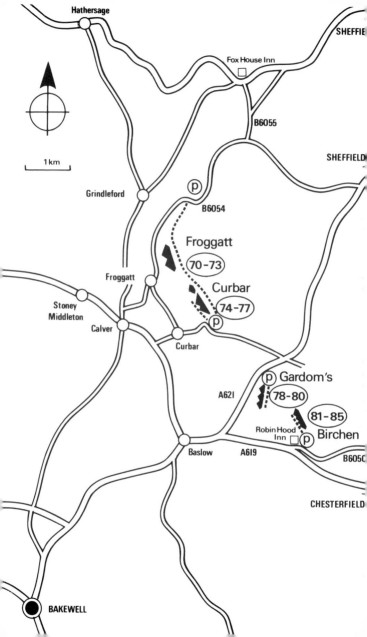

70: FROGGATT – CAVE AREA

Summary: Crack climbs, from finger to chimney width, on a popular and pleasantly situated outcrop. An unprotected slab provides a contrast.

Crag Conditions: Faces south-west and west at 275m, so conditions can be good at any time of year. Trees below the crag do not significantly impede drying, though midges can be a problem on calm days. Very popular during weekends and summer evenings.

Approach: Initially via the A625 Hathersage to Sheffield road. Turn off at the Fox House Inn on the B6055, then turn right soon after on the B6054 to Calver. Large car park on the right (GR:256 777), 3km/2 miles from the Fox House (refer to the map for a southern approach). From a gate a few hundred metres down the road towards Calver (limited parking), branch left and follow a track along the escarpment top. Beyond a second gate, and after leaving trees behind, the distinctive summit of Froggatt Pinnacle comes into view. Scramble down Pinnacle Gully between pinnacle and edge to the foot of the crag. GR:249 763. 20 minutes. The Cave area is about 100m to the left (refer to Section 71 crag diagram for location).

A faster but less pleasant approach ascends from below by a path starting a short distance down the road from the Chequers Inn (limited lay-by parking further down the road at a bend).

The impressive Swimmers' Chimney splits the buttress right of Froggatt Cave, striking terror into the hearts of reluctant chimneyists. Exits over the cave roof itself are nasty, but Hawk's Nest Crack on its left side gives a fair jamming pitch (Holly Groove (VS,4c) further left is less appealing). To the left the crag falls back into a slabby expanse climbed centrally by Sunset Slab, on the right by the thin crack of Sunset Crack, and on the left by the wide fissure of North Climb. The rock is top-quality rounded grit, providing comforting friction except on the polished holds of North Climb and Swimmers' Chimney. All routes are about 10m in length. Descend by scrambling down the gully just right of Sunset Slab, or to the right of Swimmers' Chimney.

70.1 North Climb (S) ✲
The slippery rift at the left side of Sunset Slab. The initial crack has a difficult exit left to a ledge (approached more easily by shelves from the left). Now climb the horrible, unprotected off-width crack.

70.2 Sunset Slab (VS+,4b) ✲ ✲ ✲
Beautiful slab climbing with no protection. Use a thin crack just left of Sunset Crack to get onto the main sweep of slab then climb diagonally left, via a committing move on shelving holds, to below a blanked-off flake crack. The flake improves to provide layaways for a breath-holding finish.

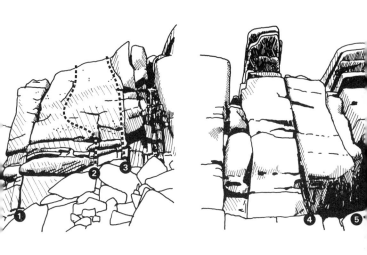

70.3 Sunset Crack (VS−,4b) ※

The protectable thin crack at the right-hand side of Sunset Slab. Hardest near the start.

70.4 Hawk's Nest Crack (VS−,4b) ※ ※

Protectable, with some good jamming moves. The crack is wide and undercut at first but soon narrows to hand width. Climb past another wide section above a chockstone to finish just right of the rock beak.

70.5 Swimmers' Chimney (VD+) ※ ※

A special treat for chimney freaks, and for others an exercise in anxiety control. The slightly converging walls are set near the limit for back-and-footing and so instil a feeling of immense insecurity. As the block approaches, the timid will start treading water and faffing around with runners, while the bold will stick to their backstroke then jam over the left side of the block. The through-route exits are dark and easy, although a mischievous leader could finish up the outside (actually quite simple) and fake grunts of desperation while the runnerless rope sways in the void.

71: FROGGATT – HEATHER WALL AREA

Summary: A disparate group of climbs in pleasant surroundings, including a gently-angled jam crack, a baffling mantelshelf, and a bald slab.

Crag Conditions: As for Section 70.

Approach: As for Section 70 (refer to the diagram opposite for precise location of buttresses).

The upper part of the 15m high Heather Wall buttress lies back at a slabby angle above an undercut base. Heather Wall itself flanks the undercut via cracks up the left side, while Tody's Wall overcomes it by strange means to finish up the central bottomless crack. Further right, the blank-looking 12m of Three Pebble Slab sets a mind-stretching exercise of its own. Descend left of Heather Wall, or go right and descend Pinnacle Gully.

71.1 Heather Wall (VD) ✳ ✳ ✳
A delightful crack climb in every respect; not too steep, and generous with good jams and runners. Only the start is nasty – using a polished hold to get established on the first face crack. From the ledge above, move right to climb the upper crack and slim corner.

71.2 Tody's Wall (VS+,5b) ✳ ✳
A disjointed climb, steep then slabby, including a notorious and infuriating obstacle. Start in the depression below the undercut slab and climb up to a block below the overlap (take time to arrange protection here). Get onto the block then pivot up onto a hold on the lip (if at first you don't succeed...). The reward for perseverance is a concave slab split in its upper part by an excellent finger crack.

71.3 Three Pebble Slab (E1,5a) ✳ ✳
Despite the loss of pebbles the slab surface is now safely within modern bounds of adherence. Nevertheless, the crux is more a problem of balance than pure friction. Start on the left side of the slab and climb direct past creases (possible protection) to a prominent pocket above a slight overlap. Teeter up, balance rightwards onto a sloping foothold, then sprint for the big ledge on pure friction. Thread belay in a niche (and a quick descent to the left).

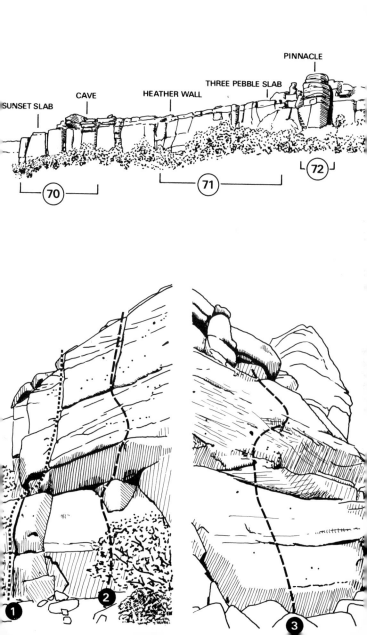

SUNSET SLAB   CAVE   HEATHER WALL   THREE PEBBLE SLAB   PINNACLE

70   71   72

Tody's Wall (71.2), Froggatt

Valkyrie (72.1), Froggatt

72: FROGGATT – FROGGATT PINNACLE

Summary: The finest of all gritstone pinnacles, climbed by a circuitous two-pitch route which calls on a wide variety of techniques for success.

Crag Conditions: As for Section 70.

Approach: As for Section 70.

There are a dozen routes up Froggatt Pinnacle, but no easy ones. Valkyrie climbs a crack on the west face, traverses a break to a stance on the south-west arete, and finishes up the wrinkled nose above: 20m of superb climbing. Descend by abseil down the short north side from an *in situ* ring bolt.

72.1 Valkyrie (HVS,5a) ✳ ✳ ✳
One of the top-ten gritstone classics. The climbing is nowhere easy, and the outcome remains in doubt until the leader is high on the second pitch. Good protection from double ropes. Jam the slanting crack on the west face to the break (4c). Hand-traverse right on jams and pull onto a belay ledge on the south-west arete (4c). Gain a short vertical crack on the right (runners) then move boldly left and balance round onto the nose above the stance (crux). Climb more easily up wrinkled rock to the top.

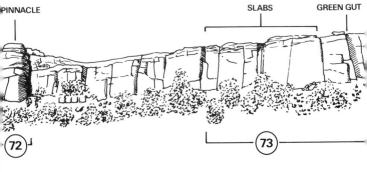

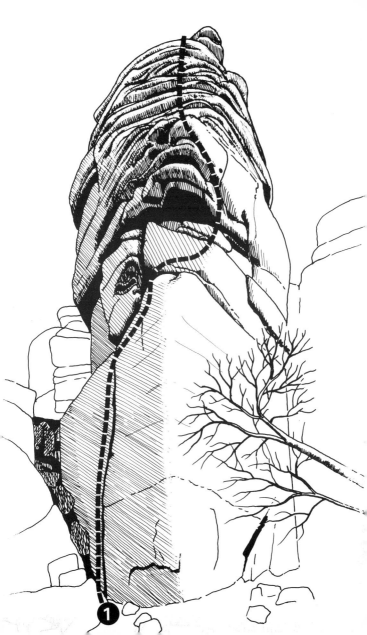

73: FROGGATT – SLABS AREA

Summary: Minor slab routes and   **Approach:**   As for Section 70.
a superb corner.

Crag Conditions: As for Section
70.

Sections of the edge have been quarried here, so holds are more square-cut
than usual. Route lengths range from 12-14m. Descend the break (M) just right
of Trapeze, or more easily well beyond Green Gut. (Refer to Section 72 for
location of buttresses.)

73.1 Slab Recess (D) ✳
Climb to a narrow ledge and move left. Layback a gritty flake and exit left.

73.2 Allen's Slab (S) ✳
Climb past the narrow ledge of 73.1 and follow a rising foot line rightwards.
Traverse right with a crease for both hands and feet to finish near Trapeze
Direct. Spaced protection.

73.3 Trapeze (VD) ✳
Climb the crack to a bulge then swing right to a shelf. Finish just left of the
descent break.

73.4 Trapeze Direct (VS–,4b) ✳
Pull over the bulge of 73.3 with a long reach to a more-or-less jammed chock.

73.5 Green Gut (S+) ✳ ✳ ✳
Ignore the name: this is a great line, clean and sustained, climbed on jams and
polished bridging holds with good protection.

Green Gut (73.5), Froggatt

74: CURBAR – ELIMINATE WALL

Summary: A famous and intimidating gritstone classic, combin-
ing jamming and chimneying
techniques.

Crag Conditions: South-west
facing at 325m in a wind-exposed
setting. Dries quickly after rain. There
are fewer good routes in the lower
and middle grades than at Froggatt,
so the crag is generally less popular.

Approach: From the A623 Stoney
Middleton to Baslow road. Turn off at
Calver on the minor road to Curbar
village. Ignore junctions to left and right
and continue rising steeply beyond the
village until the crag comes into view
high on the left. Park after an S-bend at
a series of lay-bys (GR:259 748). Take
the path by the wall, cross a stile, then
go diagonally left to the crag. GR:258
75l. 10 minutes.

Three prominent cracks split Curbar's vertical and once-quarried 18m
Eliminate Wall: Left Eliminate (E1,5c), The Peapod and Right Eliminate (E3,5c).
The Peapod is by far the most appealing. Despite weathering, the cracks and
face holds are still comparatively square-cut and sharp. A silvery green lichen
gives the rock an unhealthy complexion, but it proves to be clean and sound.

74.1 The Peapod (HVS,5b) ✳ ✳ ✳

Much less accommodating than suggested by photographs, though
protection restores some of the lost sense of security. The slanting entry crack
is too thin for hands and feet so polished wall holds must support a grab for the
base of the pod. A thin crack at the rear is too far away for handholds but,
along with a curious pocket in the right wall, accepts extended runners. The
pod's smooth side walls arch upwards and flare outwards: the bridging feels
good at first but you know it can't last. Soon the walls force a left-facing, back-
and-foot session supplemented by jams. This works well enough until you
realise the exit ledge is on the right. Resist the urge to dive and mantel, and
instead sustain the method until jams can be reached above the ledge. Even
now the exit is precarious (and the crux). From the rest ledge, climb the steep
but technically reasonable upper crack to a platform. Exit here or swing right
and finish up a short wall.

AVALANCHE WALL

BEL AMI

ELIMINATE WALL

76

75

74

1

75: CURBAR – BEL AMI AREA

Summary: A layback pitch and a corner jam crack, both requiring a bold approach.

Approach: As for Section 74. Continue 50m left to the buttress topped by a rock fin.

Crag Conditions: As for Section 74.

Three grooves cut the 10m right side of the buttress (from left to right): Maupassant, L'Horla (E1,5b) and Insanity (E2,5c). Bel Ami, route length 16m, climbs the shady corner on its left side (Green Crack (HVS,5a) climbs the right wall), to finish up the tottering fin. Descend via the break left of Bel Ami, or down a hole at the back of the ledge above Maupassant.

75.1 Maupassant (HVS,5a) ✽ ✽
A cure for layback phobias. Layback flake cracks with half-rests and protection to the final wide crack. The prospect of laybacking this is horrific, but if feels right once committed.

75.2 Bel Ami (VS–,4b) ✽ ✽
Disjointed, though the jamming is excellent. Climb the slight corner left of the 'Gents' with increasing difficulty to good runners. A final flourish on jams leads to the belay platform. Nervously climb the friable arete of the fin, then worry how to belay the second.

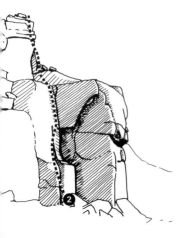

Bel Ami (75.2), Curbar

76: CURBAR – AVALANCHE WALL

Summary: A technical *HVS* face crack, plus an imposing *VS* wall climb on the shady side of Curbar's most impressive buttress.

Crag Conditions: As for Section 74. The PMC1 wall faces north-west so may be cold and damp.

Approach: As for Section 74 (refer to crag diagram for precise location).

The buttress front is split by the fierce-looking Elder Crack (E2,5b), and indented on its left side by the hanging groove of Profit of Doom (E4,6b). PMC1 climbs the sombre left wall, and Avalanche Wall the cracked left side of the quarried face further left. Both routes are about 15m long. Descend easily to the left.

76.1 PMC1 (VS–,4b) ✶ ✶
Intimidating, with spaced protection. Climb cracks just right of the corner to a ledge. A series of large flat holds now lead up to the right with more difficulty than you would suppose.

76.2 Avalanche Wall (HVS,5a) ✶ ✶
Sustained but well protected. Start up the right-hand twin crack then transfer to the left with difficulty and follow it, curving right, to the convergence. Exit strenuously to a gravel-covered terrace (risk of causing stonefall).

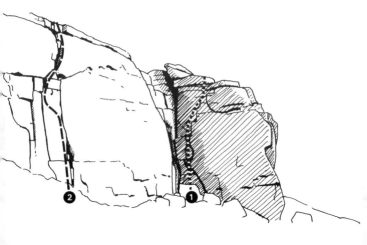

77: CURBAR – THE BRAIN AREA

Summary: Contrasting mid-grade routes on a secluded part of the edge.

Crag Conditions: As for Section 74.

Approach: Initially as for Section 74 then walk left above the crag to within 50m of where the path descends over three or four rock steps. Descend the depression between buttresses then refer to the diagram for precise locations. 20 minutes.

Sorrell's Sorrow climbs the 12m front of the protruding buttress via the undercut off-width crack above a terrace. The Brain, with 18m of climbing, finds a way up a slabby plinth then climbs a hidden corner on the right of the prow. Descend to the right from Sorrell's Sorrow, or to left or right from The Brain.

77.1 Sorrell's Sorrow (HVS,5a) ✲✲
A sadistic off-width. From the terrace, enter the undercut base of the crack and climb it past a chock with a hard move on rounded holds to gain the wide middle section. It gets worse. The next section, though easier angled, is infuriatingly smooth and is climbed by fist and arm jams supplemented by nameless udges.

77.2 The Brain (VS,4c) ✲✲
Climb the wall-angled base of the slab on the left then teeter rightwards without protection on friable holds. Ascend to the top right of the slab and gain a belay ledge right of the upper prow. Climb the corner direct, or move left at half height to finish on the arete.

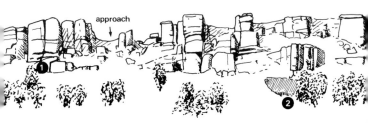

Gardom's and Birchen Edges

(Refer to the map accompanying the regional introduction to Froggatt/Curbar Escarpment on page 193.)

Of the two edges which flank the high ground above Baslow, the chain of buttresses thrust up from the trees on the nearer slope is by far the less popular. Devotees of Gardom's Edge do not complain. The crag is ideally suited for a flying visit to pick off one of its classics, be it NMC Crack at *Hard Diff,* Elliott's Buttress Direct at *VS,* Eye of Faith at *HVS,* or Moyer's Buttress at *E1.* In each case the isolation of the buttress enriches the quality of the climb.

Birchen Edge has few great climbs but many good ones. Here you will find one of the largest concentrations of quality low-grade climbing on grit. Hence its popularity. The sunny aspect, pleasant upland outlook, reclining angle, and friendly atmosphere, are all conducive to an enjoyable day's climbing. Countless gritstone apprenticeships have been served here, though the edge is equally popular with soloists feeding their insatiable appetites for grit.

Access: There are no restrictions on access to either of the crags provided they are approached as described. Dogs should be kept on a lead or, better still, left at home.

Powder Monkey Parade (81.4), Birchen

78: GARDOM'S – MOYER'S BUTTRESS

Summary: A tremendous route, with both delicate and strenuous climbing, up the front face of a secluded buttress.

Crag Conditions: West facing at 275m. Takes almost no drainage, although trees below the crag may retard drying.

Approach: Via the A621 Baslow to Sheffield road. Limited parking at a layby below the roadside buttress at the extreme north end of the crag (GR:274 738). If this is occupied, park on the verge of a minor road which branches off a few hundred metres towards Sheffield. Paths below the crag are discontinuous so approach all buttresses from the top. Cross the stile above the layby and follow a path along the escarpment top, past a second stile and through a wood. The flat top of Moyer's Buttress, identified by two blocks 1.5m and 2.5m long, is about 100m beyond the end of the wood. GR:272 733. 5 minutes.

The tall (20m) and isolated Moyer's Buttress presents the most compelling challenge on Gardom's. The front face is divided by a roof into a smooth base and a wrinkled upper wall. Stormbringer (E3,5c) takes the left edge of the front face via a mantelshelf above the roof, while the original Moyer's Buttress climbs cracks on the right-hand side until forced by the roof briefly onto the right wall before regaining the front face. The slightly overhanging right wall is taken in its entirety by Perfect Day (E5,6b). The rock is typical, well-weathered grit. Descend to the left.

78.1 Moyer's Buttress (E1,5b) ✳ ✳ ✳
The crux involves both strenuous and delicate climbing, and demands a degree of commitment beyond good protection. Ascend the easy and tired crack to the roof then dodge right to the jammed block on the south-west nose (runners). Move boldly up the right wall then teeter round onto a high, sloping foothold on the left arete (crux). Partially protected by runners in flared horizontal cracks, climb the upper wall via a difficult mantel and an easing finish on pinches.

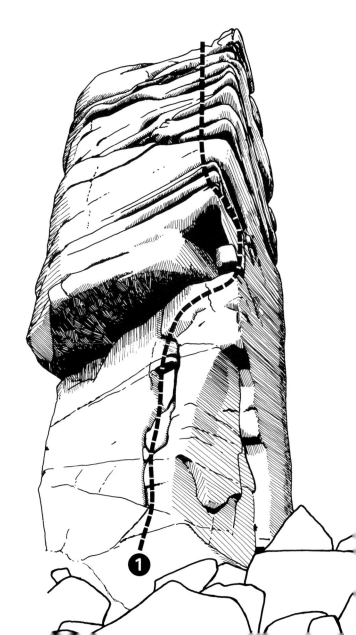

79: GARDOM'S – ELLIOTT'S BUTTRESS

Summary: A high, compact buttress in a secluded setting climbed by the original, slightly flawed *VS* and a superb *HVS* arete.

Crag Conditions: As for Section 78.

Approach: As for Section 78. Elliott's Buttress is about 30m right (south) of Moyer's.

A missing block at the foot of Elliott's Buttress prevents a direct approach to the front arete, forcing a devious entry from Eye of Faith. The Direct takes the easier-looking right face, only to find its exit obstructed by a bulging headwall. Elliott's Buttress Indirect (VS,4c) climbs the corresponding face on the left, but is not so interesting. Both described routes are about 20m long. Descend by the left-bounding gully.

79.1 Eye of Faith (HVS,5b) ✳ ✳ ✳
Acrobatic climbing up the arete. Good protection at the overhang, then spaced. Start up the roof-capped corner then struggle left (or, more logically, creep in from the gully on the left and reduce the overall grade to 5a). A block and crack for finger jams and runners point the way over the overhang. Above, move right onto the arete and climb the edge by a layaway sequence (protection coming soon) to a ledge. There's a tricky move to start the top arete but the rest is simple.

79.2 Elliott's Buttress Direct (VS,4c) ✳ ✳
Mostly straightforward but obstructed by the final wall (the arete finish reduces the standard to VS-,4b). Good climbing, though flawed by the broken area at half height. Start on the right side of the buttress front, just left of an evil-looking chimney/gully. Layback the slim corner in two stages then, ignoring easy ground to the right, climb a pleasant face crack to a ledge. A smooth, bulging wall bars entry to the final crack. This can be overcome direct, or by doglegs to left or right. By any route this is 4c climbing on rounded handholds. A better alternative, more in keeping with the lower section, is to move left and climb the arete, initially by a tricky move but then on good holds for a superb finish.

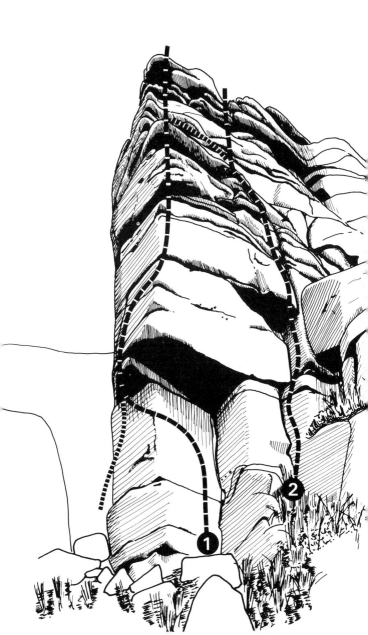

80: GARDOM'S – APPLE BUTTRESS

Summary: An isolated and secluded buttress climbed by low-grade routes, one of them the best *Diff* on the edge.

Crag Conditions: As for Section 78. The buttress stands clear from the trees and so dries quickly. However, NMC Crack takes the north side of the prow so may remain damp for longer.

Approach: Initially as for Section 78. A wall cuts across the path about 500m beyond the end of the wood. The fin at the top of Apple Buttress will be seen about 100m further on. 10 minutes.

Apple Buttress protrudes from the edge as a narrow prow topped by a fin-like block. The narrow front face – Apple Arete (VS,4b) – is bounded on the right by the block-filled fissure of Apple Crack. The left wall of the prow is cut by the prominent slanting line of NMC Crack. These routes are about 15m long. Arranging the top belay requires some ingenuity if the final cracks are included. There's a quick descent to the left. (The grooved wall left of Apple Buttress contains several short *VS* climbs, and there are several obvious *S* to *VS* miniatures in the area.)

80.1 NMC Crack (D+) ✳ ✳ ✳
An excellent climb based on the flake crack which splits the left wall of the prow. Sustained but fair, and protectable. Semi-layback the initial crack then mantel onto a ledge below a steeper section. The crack in the corner is disconcertingly wide but there's a helpful subsidiary crack on the right wall. Ignore an escape opportunity from the platform above, and jam the slanting crack onto the crest of the prow.

80.2 Apple Crack (D+) ✳
A bit of a let-down after NMC Crack, but still worthwhile. Overcome an awkward start by a long reach to a block, then plod up the wide crack to a big ledge on the right of the fin. Escape here or, as on NMC Crack, climb a crack to finish on the prow (this one has an awkward exit, so don't rush).

81: BIRCHEN — TRAFALGAR WALL

Summary: A variety of popular low-grade climbs, including a poorly-protected slab and a classic buttress. lower grades, and for this reason the crag is extremely popular.

Crag Conditions: Faces south-west at 300m. Clean and therefore dries quickly. The rock is well-weathered and rounded, though generally set at an easier angle than usual for grit. It is generously supplied with ledges, cracks and chimneys. The best routes are in the

Approach: From the A619 Baslow to Chesterfield road. A little over 1.5km/1 mile from Baslow, turn left on the B6050 and park near the Robin Hood Inn (GR:281 721). Walk up the road a short distance then cross a stile on the left and follow a path rising to the crag, arriving near Nelson's Monument. GR:279 729. 20 minutes.

To the right of the monument are three linked buttresses and a slabby wall. An undercut base to the slabby wall provides a sharp test of commitment on all its routes. The right-hand of the three buttresses is climbed by Powder Monkey Parade, raised to classic status by an overhung entry from the left. The Chain and The Promenade start on the left-hand buttress but finish on the central one for added length. Route lengths range from 10-15m.

81.1 Trafalgar Wall (VD+) ✳
A trying lead but a cruise for seconds – provided they can get off the ground. Pull awkwardly onto the rightmost of the ledges then climb the unprotected slabby wall on sloping holds, finishing with a thought-provoking move onto the rounded top.

81.2 Trafalgar Crack (D) ✳
Finds the easiest way up the slabby wall. Beginners (and others) can be demoralised by the hard start. Pull onto a ledge 1m left of Trafalgar Wall and follow the ramp leftwards. Large nuts protect occasional jamming moves between conventional holds on the wide finishing crack. (The thin crack of Barnacle Bulge (S) can be used as a direct start to the wide crack.)

81.3 Camperdown Crawl (S+) ✳
Climbs the left side of the slabby wall with a desperate start and a delicate finish. Finger-jam the thin crack 3m right of the left edge to an easement (4c) then climb direct up the delicate slab to a rounded finish.

81.4 Powder Monkey Parade (S) ✳ ✳ ✳
One of the best routes on the edge. Double ropes are useful to protect the second. Surmount the chockstone in the left-bounding V-cleft with great difficulty. Now move up 2m to horizontal slot (runners) and use it to traverse boldly rightwards onto the face below the overhang. Continue hand-traversing on a good edge until footholds arrive. Step up at a crack at the end of the

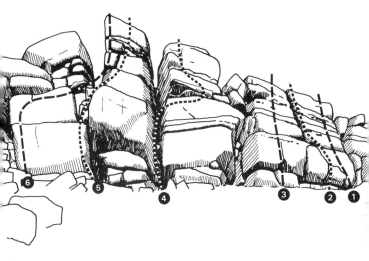

overhang (runners), then move left onto a ledge below the top arete. Climb this without protection or undue difficulty to the top. Good belay anchors are difficult to arrange here.

81.5 The Chain (VD) ✳

The middle buttress is undercut by a small cave. Exit left from the cave onto a polished slab and pull onto blocks. From a higher ledge on the right, traverse right onto the buttress front and climb it to the top.

81.6 The Promenade (M) ✳

Wandering but worthwhile. Climb the left side of the slabby base of the left-hand buttress to an overhang then traverse right to gain the blocks of The Chain. The cleft above provides an easy finish, though the exposed arete to its right is better.

82: BIRCHEN – MONUMENT AREA

Summary: Exciting mid-grade buttress routes. A chimney and a V-corner add variety.

Crag Conditions: As for Section 81.

Approach: As for Section 81.

This group consists of two large buttresses and a smaller one sandwiched between. The right-hand buttress, topped by the monument, is unusually steep for this crag – hence the difficulty of Orpheus Wall (HVS,5b) up its front face. The major routes condense a lot of interest into a meagre 10m length.

82.1 Monument Chimney (D) ✳
Not a chimney at all but a straightforward bridging groove.

82.2 Topsail (VS–,4b) ✳ ✳
A one-move wonder, but what a move! Climb the polished crack to a good resting place below the overhang (runners). Reach over for a good flake edge and use it to get established on the easy upper slab.

82.3 Sail Chimney (VD) ✳ ✳
The clean, classic chimney left of Topsail.

82.4 Sail Buttress (S) ✳ ✳ ✳
Start under the overhang and find jams for the semi-mantel out right. Now traverse impressively left using pockets and a horizontal crack to a foothold on the arete. Finish more easily up the arete.

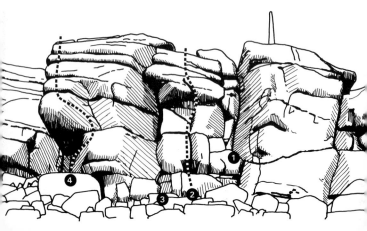

83: BIRCHEN – PORTHOLE BUTTRESS

Summary: Diverse problems, from mantelshelves to squeeze chimneys.

Crag Conditions: As for Section 81.

Approach: As for Section 81.

Left of the monument an undercut slab breaks up into two buttresses separated by a deep cleft. All routes are around 12m high.

83.1 Nelson's Slab (S) ✳
Pull onto the hanging ledge at the right side of the undercut (best entered from the right). Move left to the centre of the slab and climb it to finish at a slot.

83.2 Porthole Direct (S) ✳✳
A delicate initial wall and slim groove lead to a ledge. The overhanging crack above left has good jams and runners but demands commitment at the first bulge.

83.3 Captain's Crawl (M) ✳
Climb easily up the gully to the cave then find a way out left – a tight squeeze, but there's daylight at the end of the tunnel.

83.4 Captain's Bunk (S+) ✳
Climb the left-hand buttress by three mantelshelves: the first (and crucial one) via a hold on the right; the second uneventfully; and the third with protection.

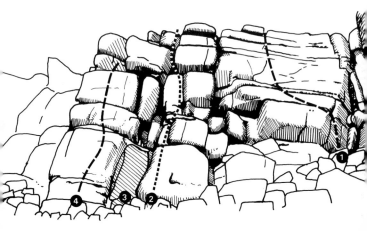

84: BIRCHEN – CROW'S NEST AREA

Summary: A varied collection of mostly *Severe* routes. Chimneys, cracks, grooves and bald slabs are all represented.

Crag Conditions: As for Section 81.

Approach: As for Section 81.

The Crow's Nest area defines the left extremity of the worthwhile climbing on the edge. As elsewhere, it has been split into a series of slender buttresses by a set of vertical fissures – some narrow, some wide. After a devious start the left-hand buttress front is taken by The Crow's Nest. The big chimney to its right is The Funnel, while the other routes climb the various cracks and grooves to the right. Route lengths range from 10-12m.

84.1 Emma's Dilemma (S) ✳
The crack eases after an awkward start, but there's a difficult final jamming move over a bulge (protectable).

84.2 Victory Gully (S) ✳
Pull over the chock in the clean chimney and continue up the cracked groove with a hand-rasping jam to reach to better holds.

84.3 Victory Crack (S) ✳ ✳
Good, dynamic climbing. Start up the chimney of Victory Gully then step left onto a broad ledge. Finish up the intimidating hanging crack above – sustained but protectable.

84.4 Kiss Me Hardy (VD+) ✳
Start as for The Funnel to the ledge, then pull into a narrow chimney by a gymnastic move on pockets. Now face right and, if you can, enter the slit for some unprotected but secure climbing (if not, the climbing is unprotected and insecure). Holds arrive on the right edge later.

84.5 The Funnel (D) ✳ ✳
An excellent, uncomplicated route. Climb the balancy right wall of the cracked lower corner to a ledge (or layback the corner direct). Move left to enter the chimney proper and climb it, facing left or right, to finish on the right.

84.6 The Crow's Nest (VS–,4c) ✳
A series of contrived, if interesting, problems. Strenuous and safe, then delicate and serious. Struggle up the crack on the left (4c) then, ignoring the easy escape, traverse onto the buttress front with difficulty and climb it delicately to the top (4a/b).

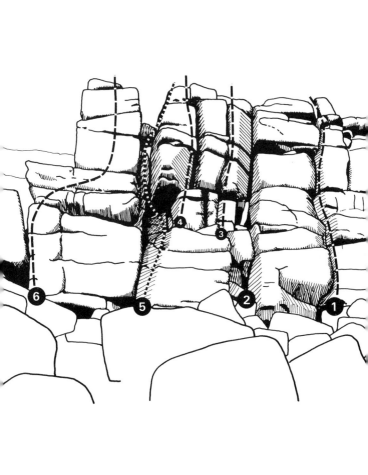

The Funnel (84.5), Birchen

85: BIRCHEN – KISMET BUTTRESS

Summary: A secluded, isolated buttress climbed by one of the finest routes on the edge.

Crag Conditions: As for Section 81. The corner takes some drainage so will take longer to dry.

Approach: As for Section 81. From the monument area, follow an increasingly indefinite path right-wards below the edge for about 300m.

The buttress consists of a central, overhung corner flanked by lesser features on which several good problems and miniature routes can be found. Horatio's Horror and Nelson's Nemesis both climb the corner then dodge the top roof to left and right respectively. Both routes are about 15m long.

85.1 Horatio's Horror (S) ✳
Let down by an inferior finish, but still worthwhile. Climb the corner crack to the roof then make a long stride left to an easy layback. Move right onto a ledge after a couple of metres and finish direct.

85.2 Nelson's Nemesis (S+) ✳ ✳ ✳
Excellent climbing with a big 'feel'. Climb the corner crack to the roof then swing right onto a good foothold (exposed). Finish up the crack in the front face.

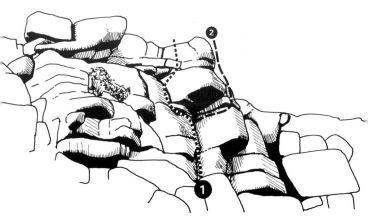

Matlock Area

The Matlock area is predominantly limestone country, of walled hillocks and steamy dales. No sign here of the windswept moors of northern grit.

Among mild-mannered countryside, Cratcliffe Tor shyly hides itself in a wood, as if it wasn't meant to be there at all. The shock of arriving at the crag to discover a 25m wall of plumb-vertical gritstone is therefore all the greater. It doesn't help to know that the route up it is called Suicide Wall.

The stubborn Black Rocks seen sticking out of the hill above Cromford are the last defiant gesture of the gritstone medium in the south-east. The buttresses look as though they have been stood for too long in the sun, their once angular forms melted into cindery globs. Route-baggers come here primarily to climb on Birch Tree Wall, possibly because it catches the sun and so has been photographed to good effect. Yet equally good routes await among the trees and slimy gloom of the north face: some hard, like the slippery Lean Man's Climb; some easy, like the inside route of Queen's Parlour Chimney; and some almost beyond belief, like Stonnis Arete.

The final route selected for this group has nothing in common either with Cratcliffe Tor or Black Rocks. Dukes Quarry, a dripping and ivy-choked hole in the earth, could be used as a film set for *Tarzan and the Giant Ants*. You may wonder why you have been brought here, until the blindfold is removed and, blinking at the rush of light, you gaze up at the Great Crack. If the crack is dry then you will believe your life's destiny was to be brought to such a crack on such a day.

Access: To preserve continuing access to Cratcliffe Tor it is important to approach the crag only as described. Dukes Quarry is on private land and there is no standing permission to climb. However, the paths into the quarry appear to be in regular use. There are no restrictions on access to Black Rocks. Dogs should be kept on a lead or, better still, left at home.

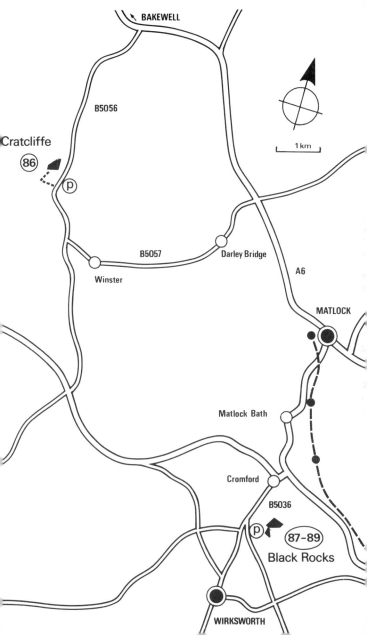

86: CRATCLIFFE TOR – SUICIDE WALL

Summary: A strong contender for the best *HVS* on grit. Climbs a system of cracks on the high, vertical face of a tree-shrouded crag.

Crag Conditions: Faces south-east at 225m. Trees at the base of the crag inhibit drying. The rock in the lower part is lichenous, and often damp with seepage. Midges can be a problem in late spring and summer. Idyllic on crisp sunny days in spring or autumn. There are few good routes in the lower and middle grades, though a concentration of quality *Extremes* ensures a degree of popularity.

Approach: Refer to the access notes in the regional introduction. Approach initially via the A6 Bakewell to Matlock road. From Bakewell, turn right after about 3km/2 miles onto the B5056 to Ashbourne. The crag will be seen on the right above trees after about 4km/2.5 miles. From Matlock, turn left after about 3km/2 miles onto the B5057 to Darley Bridge and Winster. Continue past Winster village then turn right onto the B5056 to Bakewell. The crag will be seen on the left above trees after about 1.5km/1 mile. Limited roadside parking at GR:229 619, on the Bakewell side of the track leading to the house below the tor (avoid blocking gates etc.). Do not attempt to approach the crag direct. Instead, leave the track where it bends right towards the house and follow a path veering slightly left towards the pinnacles of Robin Hood's Stride. Shortly before reaching them, enter the wood on the right and follow the path rightwards to the crag, passing the Hermit's Cave, to the huge V-corner of Owl Gully. GR:228 623. 15 minutes.

On arrival the most obvious feature of the crag is the deep recess of Owl Gully (a D+ which looks easy and awful but proves to be awkward and quite interesting). The side walls of Owl Gully are impressive: Fern Hill (E2,5c) traverses out left from halfway up Owl Gully then follows a slanting crack to the arete before dodging a top overhang on the right; while the more difficult Five Finger Exercise (E2,5c) takes the right wall, finishing up a hanging flake. Round to the right, on the far side of the huge prow, a tree grows out of a cave at one third height – The Bower. Suicide Wall climbs the 25m face to its right – one of the biggest on grit. The rock is characterised by pockets and flake cracks. The usual descent is by the gully to the right of the wall.

86.1 Suicide Wall (HVS,5a/b) ✳ ✳ ✳
A magnificent route, at the upper limit of its grade, based on the series of face cracks in the vertical wall right of The Bower. Sustained and tiring. Feels serious despite good protection. Start below a gnarled tree growing out of the rock a few metres up the wall. Climb the overhanging chimney on the right (or traverse diagonally right into it from the tree) then go diagonally left above the

tree to a shallow niche. Climb the difficult narrow-hand crack slanting slightly left to a welcome rest at a boss of rock (traverse left for an optional belay in The Bower). When ready, stride right from horizontal jams and pull up using a good but small face hold to gain a difficult flake crack, climbed on improving holds to a large niche. Step left and boldy layback (or awkwardly jam) the wide flake crack on an improving edge to below the final bulge. Step right and pull over on good holds.

87: BLACK ROCKS – BIRCH TREE WALL

Summary: Two obstinate *VS* routes on the rounded rock of a very public face.

Crag Conditions: West facing at 275m. Unaffected by trees and dries quickly. Can be hot in high summer, but a welcome refuge from the dank north face on sunny afternoons in autumn or spring. Black Rocks are a popular venue with both climbers and tourists, so the area is especially busy during summer weekends (midweek brings no peace as the noise from the nearby quarry takes over). The rock is rough and sound but extremely rounded, sometimes gritty and, in places, highly polished.

Approach: Take the A6 south from Matlock then, soon after passing through Matlock Bath, turn right onto the A5012. Turn left after 200m onto the B5036 through Cromford. When rising out of the village, the crag will be visible high up on the left. Turn left in about 1 km/0.5 mile on a minor road signposted 'Black Rock' and take the second left on a track leading to the upper of two large car parks. Birch Tree Wall lies just a few minutes away up the hill. GR:293 557.

Birch Tree Wall stands at right-angles to the main line of crags and, incongruously, above a mound of limestone scree. At its right end are several short problem routes, including an ancient chipped slab which even grown-ups can enjoy. The first obvious line is the short cleft of South Gully (D, but with harder variant finishes to left and right). The next obvious feature is the shallow cave below the centre of the wall. Lone Tree Gully (VD+) climbs direct to the top, while Lone Tree Groove 'escapes' up the left-slanting (and treeless) groove. Birch Tree Wall takes the crack in the big wall on the left until forced off to the left. The hanging right arete of the large boulder at the left end of the wall is laybacked by Curving Arete (E5,6b) while, should you be interested, the hanging groove to its left is climbed by Gaia (E8,7a). Both described routes are about 20m long. There's a simple descent to the right of the wall.

87.1 Lone Tree Groove (VS–,4c) ✳ ✳
A pleasant groove with a puzzling entry. From the niche above the cave, thread a chock in the left-slanting groove then struggle into it (probably facing right and jamming). The middle and upper sections of the groove are delightfully simple.

87.2 Birch Tree Wall (VS+,5a) ✳ ✳
A demanding route with a technical start and an exposed exit traverse. Large nuts and double ropes are useful. Enter the crack with difficult moves on shiny pocket holds, continue with conviction up the widening crack and then exit left onto a large ledge (alternatively, start up a thin crack 2m left then balance right at 3m into the widening crack). From the ledge, traverse left across the break

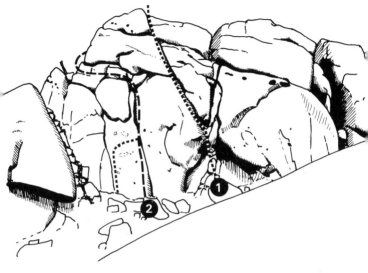

(4b) and pull round to easy ground on the left side of the top wall (to protect the second on the traverse, find belay anchors well back over the crag top and take a stance above the upper wall).

Lone Tree Groove (87.1), Black Rocks

Stonnis Arete (88.3), Black Rocks

88: BLACK ROCKS – STONNIS ARETE AREA

Summary: A tough *VS* layback and a unique *V.Diff* friction arete on gloomy north-facing buttresses.

Crag Conditions: Refer to Section 87 for general comments. North facing, and therefore often cold and greasy. Grit and lichen can be a problem, and the initial crack of Lean Man's seeps drainage after bad weather. Stonnis Arete must be absolutely dry otherwise the friction arete will be horrific. Spared the public attention of Birch Tree Wall.

Approach: As for Section 87 (refer to the diagram opposite for precise location).

Lean Man's Climb ascends the 18m tower at the right-hand side of the North Face, initially by a flake layback in its slabby base. The easy-angled Stonnis Arete (approached via the blocky face below and extended by an easy finish for a total 30m of climbing) bounds the left side of this recess, while Stonnis Crack climbs the short crack at the rear. The huge prow left of Stonnis Arete is girdled from right to left by the Promontory Traverse (HVS,5b). Descend well to the left or right of the rocks, or down the gully left of the Promontory (M).

88.1 Lean Man's Climb (VS+,5a) ✽ ✽
A precarious layback start is rewarded by good crack climbing above. Large nuts useful. Layback the prominent flake crack (with feet 'slip-slidin' away') to saplings and grass ledges (5a). Climb the cracked upper wall until it is possible to move left for a fine finish up the prominent jamming crack (4c).

88.2 Stonnis Crack (S+) ✽
Short but sweet. Climb the crack and exit left with optimism and skill (crux) to finish easily as for Stonnis Arete.

88.3 Stonnis Arete (VD) ✽ ✽ ✽
A classic grit *Diff* with the power to instil lasting terror on the uninitiated. A varied approach to the unprotected arete adds interest, though the route is flawed by an anti-climactic finish. Climb cracked blocks at the toe of the buttress to a ledge on the left. Go up the face of the hanging block, passing a creaking flake, to a poised boulder at the base of the arete. Get onto the arete as soon as possible and friction up it between occasional holds (or struggle up it *à cheval*) to the rock bay. Belay. Finish easily.

89 QUEEN'S PARLOUR

88 STONNIS ARETE   LEAN MAN'S

87 BIRCH TREE WALL

89: BLACK ROCKS – QUEEN'S PARLOUR

Summary: Chimney routes on a dark, north-facing buttress, plus an exquisite bouldering slab.

Crag Conditions: Refer to Section 87 for general comments. North facing and therefore often cold and greasy, though compensated by the added seclusion.

Approach: Initially as for Section 87 (refer to the Section 88 crag diagram for precise location). For the Railway Slab, a south-facing slab of ankle-twisting height, descend direct from Queen's Parlour to the course of the dismantled railway and follow it left until within about 100m of the car park.

The most significant feature of Queen's Parlour buttress is a large roof at half height – the underside of a huge block. The fissure to its right is the Chimney; the wider one to its left, the Gully. Above the block is a terrace from which the routes either escape or find hard variant finishes. Both routes are about 25m long. The quickest descent is to the left.

89.1 Queen's Parlour Chimney (M to VD+) ✳ ✳
A chimney with hidden depths. Start up a subsidiary rib left of the Gully line, traverse right beneath an overhang, then ascend diagonally right on scooped holds to the chimney. The Inside Route emerges onto the terrace through a hole then escapes left. Alternatively, back-and-foot the awesome bottomless chimney of the Outside Route (VD) and rejoin the Inside Route above a chockstone. An optional exit from the terrace jams the groove above the hole then chest-traverses left to finish (VD+).

89.2 Queen's Parlour Gully (D) ✳
A more consistent climb than the Chimney, if less impressive. Start as for the Chimney then jam and bridge a corner to beneath the upper of two overhangs. Step right (exposed) and move up to a ledge below the wide chimney slot. Either climb the wide right-hand crack and exit right onto the terrace, or take the narrow left-hand crack (hard) and finish direct.

89.3 Railway Slab (VS,4c or 5a) ✳
Delectable slab climbing on polished holds. 8m high, but unprotected and therefore usually soloed. The right-hand route – a line of polished friction pockets – is 4c, whereas the left-hand route – which after a precarious start aims for a finger crack – is 5a. If either of these problems seems too easy then you are invited to climb up the middle at 5c.

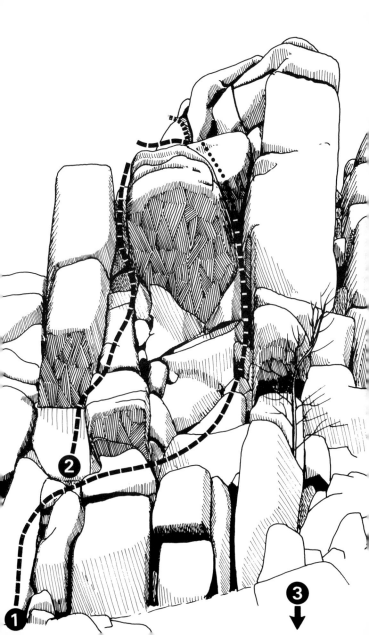

90: DUKES QUARRY – GREAT CRACK

Summary: A compelling face crack rising from the Amazonian depths of a quarry.

Crag Conditions: West facing at 125m. Trees above and below the quarry retard drying on a face that already suffers badly from drainage. Midges are a problem in late spring and summer, so the best time to come is after a dry spell in autumn.

Approach: Refer to the access notes in the regional introduction. Take the A6 south from Matlock and, just after bridging the Derwent near Whatstandwell, turn left onto the B5035 to Crich. Turn left again almost immediately for Holloway on a narrow lane. Park after about 300m where a track bears down to the left (room for 2 cars). Beyond wooden posts opposite, tracks slant left and right. Follow the right-hand track for about 100m then break off left, up the bank, and follow a path along a trough to the quarry (here short and broken). Continue on the path, curving right, to approach the base of a big wall. GR:334 545. 10 minutes.

Two ragged cracks split the left side of the 25m high Great Wall. The left-hand crack is the vividly named Woodlice Crack (VS,4c), which doesn't quite succeed in escaping the clutches of the jungle creepers. The line to its right is the depilated Great Crack which, though it could use a good wipe, is fit to climb. Descend by abseil.

90.1 Great Crack (VS+,5a) ✵ ✵ ✵
A sustained face crack, varying in width from narrow to wide hand. A must for quarry fans. There are good rests between difficult sections, of which there are several. Good protection from medium and large nuts. Even when the route is in condition, the first four difficult metres of narrow crack are likely to be slimy. So if you can get up this section you should – in theory – be able to climb the remainder. Sustained jamming then leads to a niche, which is less helpful than it could have been. Escape it with some bold outside bridging and layback/jam the sharp-edged crack above. The line runs out at a small ledge, but there's another crack on the left in which two doomed saplings struggle for survival. Above, the climbing eases past blocks to a gritty finish with a huge tree belay beckoning. Don't rush it!

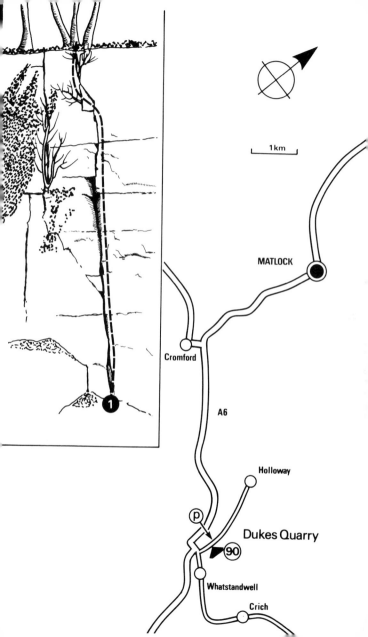

1km

MATLOCK

Cromford

A6

Holloway

℗

Dukes Quarry

90

Whatstandwell

Crich

Roaches and Hen Cloud

Between Buxton and Leek, where Staffordshire nips into Derbyshire for a bit of Peak District, gritstone country has one final stab at staging a moorland drama. Some say the Roaches and Hen Cloud are better than Stanage, better than anywhere. The climbs are big for gritstone. 20m is typical, and some are as long as 30m. But it is the variety which is so appealing: from the overhanging beaks on Ramshaw, to the fortress walls on Hen Cloud; from the scoured cracks of the Lower Tier, to the juggy pockets of the Upper Tier.

Not many outsiders want to bother with Ramshaw, not with the abundance of better climbing so near. But the place has character so a couple of easier routes have been selected to give a taste.

Even the fortress of Hen Cloud suffers neglect through its proximity to the Roaches. In the lower and middle grades are a couple of excellent clean chimneys, and a trio of rambling buttress climbs. And at a higher standard, the major *HVS* classics of Bachelor's Left-Hand and Delstree.

Most newcomers will want to head straight for the Roaches. Here, in defiance of gravity and conformity, two contrasting tiers of rock emerge from a secret garden of trees, boulders and strange goings-on. On Raven Rock, showpiece of the Lower Tier, Valkyrie and Via Dolorosa plan separate strategies to flank the huge roof. While on the Upper Tier, Pedestal Route weaves its own magic around the roof of The Sloth. Black Velvet and Black and Tans confirm the Upper Tier as the premier crag for lower and middle grade climbing, while Saul's Crack, a famous overhang problem at the upper limit of the *VS* grade, attempts to restore the balance.

The final entry in the book belongs to the isolated Third Cloud. This is not some obscure little outcrop tagged on to make up the numbers, and it is fitting that Rubberneck and Crabbie's Crack each provide climbing as good as any on grit.

Access: There are no restrictions on access provided the crags are approached as described. Dogs should be kept on a lead or, better still, left at home.

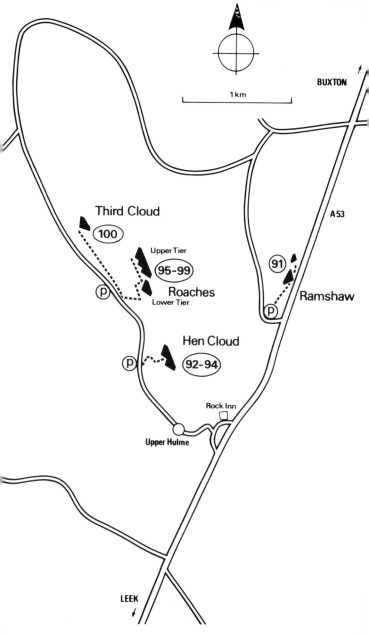

91: RAMSHAW ROCKS – PHALLIC CRACK AND BOOMERANG

Summary: Contrasting crack climbs – one overhanging the other slabby – on the strange buttresses of an accessible moorland crag.

Crag Conditions: East facing at 450m. The rock takes little drainage and so dries quickly on breezy days. Catches the morning sun so a good place to warm up before moving over to the Roaches nearby. The proximity of major crags is responsible for its relative unpopularity, though the main road below spoils the quiet.

Approach: Ramshaw Rocks overlook the A53 Buxton to Leek road about 11km/7 miles from Buxton. Turn off onto the minor road at the south end of the main group of rocks and park after 150m in a bay on the right (GR:018 619). Otherwise park on the verge of the main road and approach direct. Follow the path to the right, beneath small buttresses, to below the first big buttress – South Buttress. GR:020 623. 5 minutes. For Boomerang, continue rightwards to the next large buttress (not the lower tier).

Face routes on South Buttress weave among protruding flakes and overhangs with greater or lesser effect: Gumshoe (E2,5c) takes the left-hand face, while Battle of the Bulge (VS–,4b) and The Cannon (S+) follow the left and right lines through the less imposing central area. Phallic Crack takes advantage of the fissure cleaving the right-hand side of the face, yet it too fails to avoid a muscle-twitching entry. The warped prows of Boomerang Buttress are even more intractable, except where a slab and a wall meet at a wide crack to create the lucky line of Boomerang. The rock is rough, solid and barely polished. Both routes are about 12m long. Descents are obvious.

91.1 Phallic Crack (VD+) ✳ ✳
Thuggy climbing up an overhanging chimney/crack. Getting established on the jutting rock at 5m poses a prickly problem, so it's wise to take precautions. The crack widens above to a chimney, but there are no nasty surprises.

91.2 Boomerang (D+) ✳ ✳
An unlikely route based on a rising semi hand-traverse. Not much protection for the leader, though the second can be adequately safeguarded. Climb the wide vertical crack (crux) to a natural chock useful for protecting the second. Follow the unprotected but straightforward wide crack leftwards, supported by the comforting friction of the rough slab beneath.

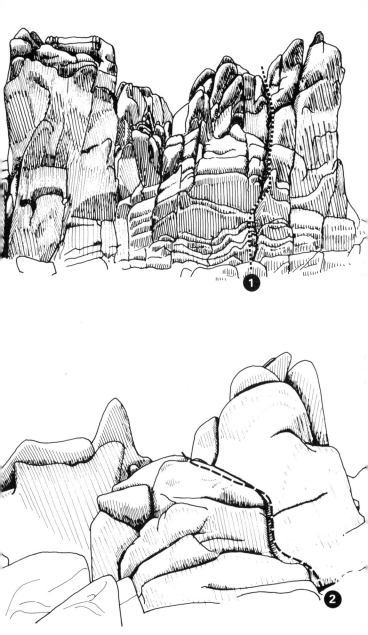

92: HEN CLOUD – BACHELOR'S AREA

Summary: A cluster of crack and chimney climbs, plus a superb hard face climb, on a towering buttress.

Crag Conditions: Faces south-west at 400m. Exposed to bad weather but dries quickly on bright, breezy days (though Rib Chimney suffers drainage). Much less popular than the nearby Roaches, despite excellent climbing.

Approach: Via the A53 Buxton to Leek road. Turn off onto the minor road leading to Upper Hulme and fork left after 200m. The lane dips to pass through a factory then rises out of the village; park on the verge after 500m, just past a gated entrance. GR:006 615. Follow the track beyond the gate then strike direct up the hillside to the crag. GR:008 616. 10 minutes.

The right-hand buttress is cut centrally by the wide Rib Chimney, and on the right by the square-cut slot of Great Chimney. Bachelor's Left-Hand works a way up the impressive face between. Hen Cloud Eliminate (HVS,5b) climbs the cracked wall left of Rib Chimney, while the unappetising green groove to its left is the line of Second's Retreat (HVS,4c). Beyond the wide Hedgehog Crack (VS–,4b) the face tapers off into the hillside. From a distance the crag appears more sharp-edged than the Roaches, though a closer approach reveals the familiar rounded holds and wide, bulging cracks. The rock is top-quality rough grit, though parts of it are liable to become lichenous over the winter. Route lengths range from 18-25m. The easiest descent is to the left.

92.1 Rainbow Crack (VS+,5a) ✳ ✳
Insecure climbing up a cracked groove. Harder than it looks. Take some big nuts! From the foot of Great Chimney, climb the ragged crack in the right wall to a ledge (4b). Go up left to the base of the wide, leaning crack and climb it by laybacking and other means.

92.2 Great Chimney (VD+) ✳ ✳
Good climbing up a clean, square-cut slot. Well protected. Jam the left-hand crack and pull out left onto the Pulpit. Step back right and continue up the narrowing crack (runners). Bridge up a little before lunging into the right-hand crack to finish, or (harder) climb the left-hand crack throughout.

92.3 Bachelor's Climb (VS–,4b) ✳ ✳
Climb the wide, bulging crack to the sloping top of the Pulpit (a belay here is traditional). Finish up Great Chimney. Alternatively, traverse left to finish up Bachelor's Left-Hand at 4c.

92.4 Bachelor's Left-Hand (HVS,5b) ✳ ✳ ✳
A magnificent face climb up the most impressive wall on Hen Cloud. Protectable. Start up a thin crack (5b) to gain the right end of a ramp which slants in from the left. Climb the narrow-hand crack above then move right with

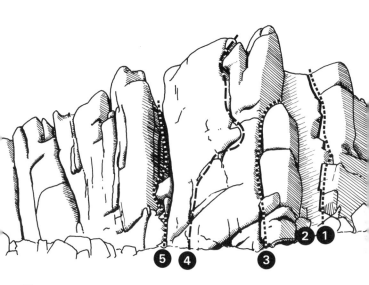

difficulty to a slanting crack. No rest here either, so pull up on a finger pocket to a flake ear, ruddy through grateful pinching (sustained 5a, crux). Rest and runners. Move right, climb a slab to its apex, then move back left to exit up the wide flake crack (4c).

92.5 Rib Chimney (VD+) ✷✷
A route to delight the chimney connoisseur. Lots of atmosphere, green rock, and apparent insecurity (protection, in fact, is untypically plentiful). Bridge awkwardly to a ledge above the initial block. Move left and climb over more blocks to the fearful upper funnel. Refrain from grovelling ineffectually up the oozing rear and instead bridge up wrinkled walls (a show of bravado made possible by good protection). Finish with a back-and-foot flourish up the narrowing chimney.

93: HEN CLOUD – CENTRAL BUTTRESS

Summary: Long, rambling climbs in the lower grades on the terraced wall of one of gritstone's highest outcrops.

Crag Conditions: As for Section 92.

Approach: As for Section 92.

Viewed frontally or in profile, the large Central Buttress appears like the outer defensive wall of a castle. No continuous lines are apparent, so the routes wander from ledge to ledge, avoiding grass and finding link pitches as best they can. This adds a mountaineering flavour to the usual gritstone diet of meat with no veg. The Arete climbs the stepped right edge of the front face, while Central Climb links a series of cracks and corners up the highest part. K2 makes the best of the rock between the two. The easiest descent is to the right of the buttress. Route lengths are around 30m.

93.1 The Arete (VD) ❊ ❊
Purists will start the arete direct with a hard mantel, while others swing in from the right. A tricky step up leads to the sloping second ledge. A wall now blunts the arete; easy at first, this is soon followed by an exposed high step to the left – unthinkable on a gusty day. The blocky remainder of the arete is simple.

93.2 K2 (VD+) ❊ ❊
Sharp problems punctuate sections of more leisurely climbing. Start up an easy corner right of the main line to gain a ledge. Climb the steep corner above the block and exit left to a large ledge. Step back right and climb the Y-crack – exposed and difficult (alternatively, jam the flake crack on the left then pull across the top of the Y-crack). Climb the constricted groove to a ledge, then finish up the easy top section of The Arete.

93.3 Central Climb (S+) ❊ ❊ ❊
Climbs the highest part of the face up a series of cracks and corners. Disjointed climbing with an expeditionary feel. The initial corner is the crux; secret, interior holds help at first, but the rounded exit is a nightmare if you get it wrong. From the left end of the ledge above, climb a corner in two stages to grass, then a deeper corner to the upper terrace. Ascend the upper wall by the cracked groove, taken direct or by one of several variant entries and exits.

94: HEN CLOUD – DELSTREE AREA

Summary: Leaning corner cracks climbed with zest or not at all. Delstree is the perfect grit *HVS*.

Crag Conditions: As for Section 92.

Approach: As for Section 92.

Left of Central Buttress the crag loses height but regains the rounded massiveness of the Bachelor's area. It is cut by a deep face crack – Main Crack (VS,4c) – and bounded on the right by the deep corner of Reunion Crack. Delstree climbs the slim groove between the two. Both described routes are about 20m long. Descend via the break to the right or, easier, right of Central Buttress.

94.1 Reunion Crack (VS,4c) ✱ ✱
An unsatisfactory line worth pursuing for the superb layback. Climb the break in the overhangs, then the slab on the right, to the impending corner. Now layback and think of England.

94.2 Delstree (HVS,5a) ✱ ✱ ✱
Magnificent bridging and jamming up a slender groove. Climb the break through the overhangs as for Reunion Crack then, after fixing runners, traverse delicately left (5a) into the base of the groove. Climb this positively, and with good runners, to the top (sustained 5a).

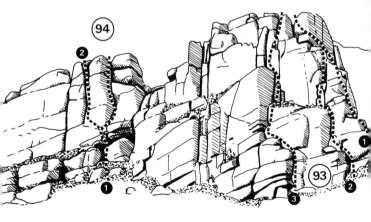

95: ROACHES LOWER TIER – RAVEN ROCK

Summary: A huge, rounded lump of grit climbed direct by a brutal *HVS* and circumspectly by the best *VS* in the region.

Crag Conditions: As for Section 96.

Approach: Initially as for Section 92. Continue past Hen Cloud and park in laybys just beyond the start of the track leading to the gap between Hen Cloud and the Roaches. GR:003 622. Walk up the track then veer left on paths passing left of Rock Hall. GR:006 622. 10 minutes.

Raven Rock is the largest of the Lower Tier buttresses seen jutting out above the trees. The upper front face is deeply undercut by a huge roof at half height. A deep corner bounds the right side of the buttress; Valkyrie starts up this corner then traverses via a huge flake onto the nose above the roof. Matinee climbs up to the flake from below and exits direct. The rock is rounded and painfully rough. Double ropes are essential on Valkyrie to protect the second and reduce drag.

95.1 Valkyrie (VS+,4c) ✳ ✳ ✳
A truly great climb, its wandering line entirely forgivable. The crux moves arrive in the position of maximum exposure, though they can be adequately protected. Bridge up the green corner at the right-hand side of the buttress and continue up the slim, cracked groove on the left (4b). Traverse left onto the fine ledge just right of the huge flake. Belay. Fix a big sling runner on the flake tip (for optimum protection of the second, clip this with the right-hand rope then use the left-hand rope for all remaining runners), then jam down the flake crack on the left almost to the lip of the roof. Balance leftwards past a bulging crack onto the buttress front (crux). Climb delicately up to a good ledge and finish in superb position up the slabby upper face.

95.2 Matinee (HVS,5b) ✳ ✳ ✳
A glorious jamming session ends in misery. Well protected. Start on a rock ledge a few metres left of the right-bounding corner of the buttress. Jam the superb twisting crack, finishing via a wider section to the Valkyrie belay (5a). Climb the continuation crack then bridge over the bulge to exit onto the sloping top by an exhausting belly wriggle (5b).

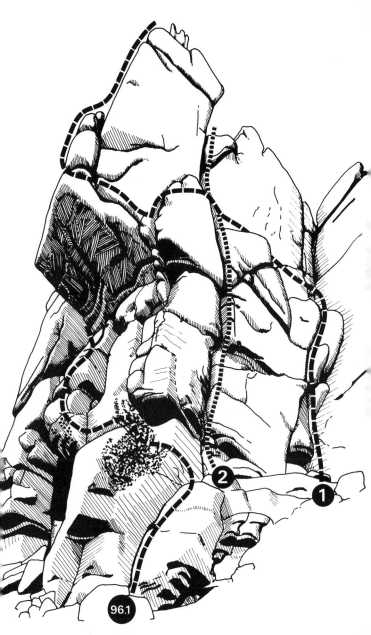

Valkyrie (95.1), Roaches

Dorothy's Dilemma (96.3), Roaches

96: ROACHES LOWER TIER – RAVEN ROCK GULLY AREA

Summary: A classic expedition up Raven Rock, plus a pair of seriously bald arete climbs.

Crag Conditions: The crag faces generally south-west at 400m. Dries reasonably well on breezy summer days, though at other times the cracks ooze for days, feeding the copious quantities of green lichen. Trees below the crag provide some shelter on windy days but retard drying even further. Less popular than the Upper Tier, though rarely empty.

Approach: As for Section 95.

The revolting interior moistness of Raven Rock Gully (D) spreads onto the side wall of Raven Rock itself, so that a lurid green slime awaits climbers on the upper part of Via Dolorosa, a 35m expedition which creeps across from a belay beneath the big roof after starting on the polished facet of slab on the right toe of the buttress. The smooth upper part of the 25m buttress left of Raven Rock Gully is climbed on its right and left edges by Bengal Buttress and Dorothy's Dilemma respectively, while Yong takes the miniature corner jam crack at the left end of the face.

96.1 Via Dolorosa (VS–,4c) ✳ ✳ ✳
A grand outing, varied and secretive. Double ropes useful. Start just right of the base of Raven Rock and trend rightwards up an off-balance polished slab (4c) to a ledge (refer to the Section 95 diagram). Stride left and struggle past the holly to a ledge. From the left end of the ledge, move up a corner then step left onto the nose and use a crack to reach a superbly positioned belay below the huge roof. Climb the narrowing slab on the left until below the huge chock of Raven Rock Gully. After fixing protection, move up to a hidden flake crack on the right (4b) and climb it to a traverse right onto the front of Raven Rock. Climb the left side of the slabby wall to the top.

96.2 Bengal Buttress (VS+,4c) ✳
A flawed line but good mental preparation for Dorothy's Dilemma. Serious. Start about 1m right of the lower left edge of the buttress and climb up via a semi-mantel to a grass ledge. Traverse the ledge rightwards then go diagonally right to the horizontal break (possible runners). Climb the delicate face just left of the edge, then step right onto the arete for the last move – an unprotected step up to the ledge (crux). Walk off here, or move left to a well-positioned flake finish and discover the best hold on the route.

96.3 Dorothy's Dilemma (E1,5a/b) ✳ ✳
Mind games up the bald left arete of Bengal Buttress. No need to queue. Start at a higher level than Bengal Buttress, below the clean part of the arete. Climb up to the break then friction up the rounded arete (possible wire protection just

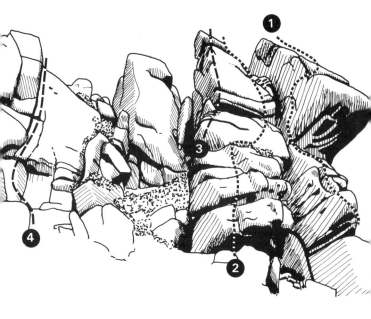

above the break). Holds improve slightly above, but there are no more runners until it's almost over.

96.4 Yong (VD+) ✲✲

A perfect miniature climb up the right-facing jamming corner just right of the steps.

97: ROACHES UPPER TIER –
PEDESTAL AREA

Summary: Excellent lower-grade climbing on one of gritstone's biggest crags.

Crag Conditions: Faces south-west at 425m. Susceptible to bad weather but dries quickly on bright, breezy days. The rock is finer grained than the Lower Tier, so pockets and juggy holds are more common. On the minus side, flakes are more likely to be friable, and the footholds polished. Extremely popular at weekends, and often busy midweek.

Approach: Initially as for Section 95. Ascend the rock staircase left of the Lower Tier then go left to below the highest part of the Upper Tier.

A huge roof at two-thirds height dominates the right-hand side of the main Upper Tier buttress. The flake crack splitting the roof above the Pedestal, a large flat-topped shield of rock, is The Sloth (HVS,5a), the most famous roof climb on grit. Pedestal Route shares some of its drama by belaying a few metres beneath. Route lengths are around 25-30m. Anchors are not always obvious among the rounded boulders above the face so it may be best to belay just below the top. The easiest descent is to the left.

97.1 Right Route (D+) ❋ ❋ ❋
A major route based on the right-bounding corner of the face. With cunning it can be adequately protected. Start by ascending large pocket holds to a ledge. Ignore the layback crack and ledge on the right, and instead climb the slabby wall to their left until beneath the overhang which leans in from the right (all very polished but protectable). Move up and left – good holds arriving – and climb up to an exit right onto the terrace (belay if required). Climb diagonally left above the ledge, suddenly exposed, and finish up the obvious crack.

97.2 Central Route (VS−,4a) ❋ ❋
Contrived, but with some good face climbing. Poor protection. Climb directly up the slabby wall midway between Right Route and the Pedestal to the horizontal break a few metres below the roof (suspect protection from wires placed behind flakes). The last move to the break is hardest, though it can be avoided on the left. Foot traverse the break rightwards onto the terrace and finish up Right Route.

97.3 Pedestal Route (VD+) ❋ ❋ ❋
The best *V.Diff* on grit? Varied climbing among impressive surroundings, marred only by the dirty finishing corner. Adequately protected, though only skilful ropework will make the best of it. Climb the steep lower wall on pockets to a shelf below the shield of the Pedestal. Semi-layback a crack on the left side of the shield to gain the Pedestal top (or climb the easier crack on its right side).

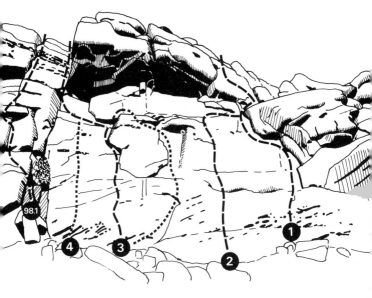

Care with belay anchors here to resist a sideways pull on the next pitch. Step down and traverse the break leftwards. A semi-mantel and reachy move up to the left gain the chimney/groove. Place a runner to redirect the rope away from a crack at the edge of the roof then pull over the small overhang and finish up the dirty corner crack (or finish diagonally across its right wall).

97.4 Technical Slab (S+) ❊ ❊

The infamous direct start to Pedestal Route – the scourge of short, nervous climbers. Not technically difficult, but there's a demoralising lack of protection. Start midway between the left-bounding chimney and the left-hand side of the Pedestal. Climb straight up the wall, steep at first and with some long reaches to pockets or edges, to gain the mid point of the traverse on Pedestal Route.

Pedestal Route, pitch two (97.3), Roaches

Pedestal Route, pitch one (97.3), Roaches

98: ROACHES UPPER TIER – JEFFCOAT'S CHIMNEY AREA

Summary: Another crop of big, adventurous climbs in the lower grades, plus a strenuous *VS* overhang.

Crag Conditions: As for Section 97.

Approach: As for Section 97.

Instead of one big roof, the left side of the main Upper Tier buttress has several smaller ones. Black Velvet and Black and Tans weave around them on the right-hand side; Jeffcoat's Chimney cleaves a way straight up the middle; while Saul's Crack escapes all but one on the left-hand side. Route lengths range from 20-30m. Belay anchors are not always obvious among the rounded boulders above the face so it may be best to belay just before reaching the top. The easiest descent is to the left.

98.1 Black Velvet (VD+) ✳ ✳ ✳
An excellent climb, often overlooked because of its better known neighbour. Good protection. Climb the chimney to the holly – the start of Hollybush Crack (VS–,4b) – then move awkwardly left onto a sloping ledge. Move left again into the base of a slim, cracked corner (on Black and Tans) and bridge and jam up it to an exit left onto a ledge. Pull over the small overlap above (runner) and climb a widening crack to the top.

98.2 Black and Tans (S) ✳ ✳ ✳
A brilliant route making the best of the buttress. Serious in the upper reaches. The desperate left-hand start is traditional but optional (double ropes advisable). Start as for Black Velvet and climb to the ledge below its overlap. Belay in the corner at the left end of the ledge. For the left-hand start, climb the polished wall 2m right of Jeffcoat's Chimney on finger flakes to the horizontal break (at least 5a), or cheat by stepping across from the chimney. A conscientious leader will now place a high runner for the second before foot traversing the break rightwards to the cracked corner of the right-hand start. From the belay, climb the corner and exit left under the overhang. Climb direct up the bulging and unprotected wall on semi-mantels – not technically difficult but requires steadiness.

98.3 Jeffcoat's Chimney (VD) ✳ ✳
An atmospheric climb which does its best to avoid the chimney. Occasional protection, lots of polish. Climb inside the chimney until forced out onto the left. From here the usual route up the left edge of the chimney is slick and unprotected, so consider the Jeffcoat's Buttress variant: stride across the chimney, traverse 2m right, climb past a flake to a glacis (runner), then swing left onto blocks above the nasty bit. Climb up to the green cave and emerge facing left – easier than it looks. With assistance from a chipped foothold, exit

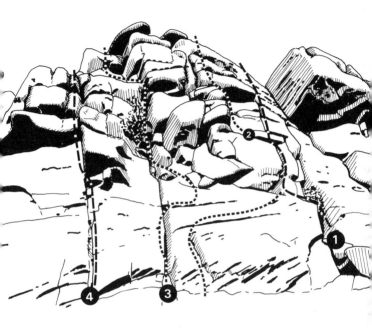

below the top block to a big ledge and thread belay – harder than it looks (sniffy purists can exit direct). Escape left or climb the overhung recessed wall above the belay, entered at 5a via the corner on the right, or at 4c with a dynamic move from the left.

98.4 Saul's Crack (VS+,5a) ✼ ✼ ✼

A safe struggle, but a struggle nonetheless. Climb the straightforward lower crack and enter a niche. Pull out left into a cracked groove and jam up it to the overhang and a partial rest. Pull over the overhang, knees thrashing, into the easing upper crack.

99: ROACHES UPPER TIER – LEFT-HAND SECTION

Summary: Minor classics in the lower grades on a less popular part of the Upper Tier.

Crag Conditions: As for Section 97. Drainage on Maud's Garden often leaves a coating of grit. However, it can be climbed in these conditions. Generally quieter than the main part of the Upper Tier (though for complete seclusion, continue left and discover the good short routes of Skyline Buttress).

Approach: As for Section 97. Continue left from the main buttress, past a large rambling crag, to prominent neighbouring buttresses undercut by roofs (that on the first at one-third height, and on the second at two-thirds height).

Maud's Garden climbs the slabby wall to the right of a corner chimney near the right side of the right-hand buttress, while Beckermet Slab swings from the chimney onto the left-bounding rib. Inverted Staircase neatly bypasses the roof of the left-hand buttress by climbing a groove to its right. The corresponding line left of the roof is the hopelessly gritty Demon Wall (S+), and so Fern Crack, which takes the cleaner undercut wall to its left, has been selected instead. Route lengths range from 18-20m. Descend to the left of either buttress.

99.1 Maud's Garden (D+) ✻
Looks tatty but has its moments. Climb the centre of the slabby wall (crux) to a crack. Ascend the crack via a ledge to the grit covered platform. Climb the chimney on the right then step left to finish up the arete.

99.2 Beckermet Slab (VD) ✻
Not technically hard but runners are few. The direct start to the arete is hopeless, so approach via slanting breaks from a couple of metres up the corner on the right. Not easy. Once on the arete, move onto a block and go up to a ledge. From the middle of the ledge, trend rightwards to the arete and finish with a delicate move to good holds.

99.3 Inverted Staircase (VD) ✻ ✻
The best climb in this group. Start below the right side of the roof and climb the slotted wall, past one awkward move, to good holds under its right-hand end. Move up to the right (runners), bridge up a shallow groove, and exit left (crux) to a large ledge and thread belay (alternatively, move left before reaching the top of the groove and pull up the wall to the ledge). From the back of the ledge, finish via a boulder-choked, bomb-bay chimney.

99.4 Fern Crack (VD) ✳

An exciting start on bulging rock but loses itself higher up. Start on an overhung ledge a few metres left of the sandy left corner of the roof. Pull up on surprising pocket holds and keep the momentum going until you can grab a projecting flake and get stood up. Move up to a ledge (thread), then trend left on curious holds to a sloping ledge on the left. From a higher ledge, walk left (thread) and finish up a dirty corner.

100: THE CLOUDS – THIRD CLOUD

Summary: Two great climbs – a *VS* jam crack and a fingery *HVS* – on an isolated and pleasantly situated buttress.

Crag Conditions: Faces south-west at 375m. Treeless, yet can be more sheltered than the Roaches. Dries quickly. The buttress is spared the crowds of the main crags.

Approach: Park as for Section 95. Go through the gate as if approaching the Roaches then turn left immediately and follow a gently rising narrow track. Ignore the right fork after 5 minutes and continue along a narrow path, passing below minor buttresses, to the compact face of the Third Cloud. GR:001 627. 10 minutes.

A grooved arete above a cave – Flower Power Arete (E1,5c) – defines the right-hand side of the front face. To its left, Crabbie's Crack twists up to a grass ledge at two-thirds height. Rubberneck climbs the thin crack rising from a shallow scoop 8m left of Crabbie's Crack. Appaloosa Sunset (E3,5c) finds a way up the left side of the intervening wall, starting near Rubberneck and utilising a high side runner. The rock – though presumably once quarried – is excellent, being more sharply cut than the Roaches Lower Tier yet less sandy and pocketed than the Upper Tier. Both routes are about 15m long. The best descent is on the left.

100.1 Crabbie's Crack (VS+,5a) ✻ ✻ ✻
A wonderful, hand-ripping crack. The optional Arete Finish – an unprotected 4c – raises the overall standard to *HVS*. Climb the initial section to a green niche. Above is a hand-width crack twisting left then right; reach it with help from a suspect block under the overlap then jam up it until forced into a right-facing layback. Exit left onto a ledge. From the higher grass ledge on the left, finish up a narrow 4b crack. For the Arete Finish, start at the base of the narrow crack and make an unprotected rising traverse to the right arete and finish with a delicate move to the top block. ✻ ✻ ✻

100.2 Rubberneck (HVS,5a) ✻ ✻ ✻
A technically absorbing climb on finger jams and face holds, reminiscent of the thin cracks at Millstone. Excellent protection where it matters. Enter the shallow scoop and climb it in an ecstasy/agony of wide bridging to reach the thin crack above (good runners here, but save room for the fingers). Pull out on finger jams and continue on improving holds to where the crack reclines. Stay with the crack as it curves left, laying-away on foot friction, but quit it soon for compact rock and adequate holds on the right. Finish up the short wall above the grass break via a thin crack or other means.

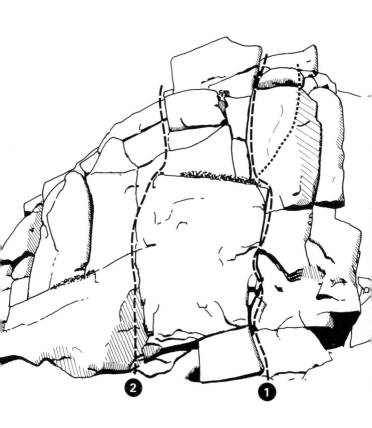

Index of Routes

CCIDENT CHECK LIST

airway using a hooked finger to remove obstructions –
, etc.
e in the recovery position (unless you suspect spinal
to maintain a clear airway.

eeding
ure from a pad to stop bleeding.

nes
asualty if a spinal injury is suspected.
actures using improvised splints and slings.

and comfortable while awaiting rescue (protect from
om cold ground).
and monitor condition regularly.

cue
mountain rescue, and try to have the following written

he injured person on the crag.
(including grid reference if possible).
accident.

until met by a police officer or member of the rescue

oment before arrival of helicopter (weight rucksacks,
es).
ising your arms in a V as helicopter approaches (do

nd of his own accord.
copter unless directed to do so by one of the crew
exhaust, etc.)

Also in the Crowood Classic Climbs series:

North Wales
Scotland – Central and Southern Highlands
Lake District
Peaks and Pennines – Limestone

A

Check Breathing
- If necessary clea
  vomit, blood, tee
- Turn casualty to
  injury). This help

Check for Severe B
- Apply direct pres
- Elevate the limb.

Check for Broken B
- Do not move the
- Immobilise other

Monitor Condition
- Keep casualty wa
  wind and insulate
- Reassure casualty

To Alert Mountain R
Dial 999, ask for police
details ready:
- Precise position of
- Location of the cra
- Time and nature of
- Extent of injuries.
- Remain by the pho
  team.

Rescue Helicopters
- Secure all loose eq
  jackets, etc. with st
- Identify yourself by
  not wave).
- Allow winchman to
- Do not approach h
  (danger from rotors

Also in the Crowood Classic Climbs series:

ACCIDENT CHECK LIST

Check Breathing
- If necessary clear airway using a hooked finger to remove obstructions – vomit, blood, teeth, etc.
- Turn casualty to lie in the recovery position (unless you suspect spinal injury). This helps to maintain a clear airway.

Check for Severe Bleeding
- Apply direct pressure from a pad to stop bleeding.
- Elevate the limb.

Check for Broken Bones
- Do not move the casualty if a spinal injury is suspected.
- Immobilise other fractures using improvised splints and slings.

Monitor Condition
- Keep casualty warm and comfortable while awaiting rescue (protect from wind and insulate from cold ground).
- Reassure casualty and monitor condition regularly.

To Alert Mountain Rescue
Dial 999, ask for police/mountain rescue, and try to have the following written details ready:
- Precise position of the injured person on the crag.
- Location of the crag (including grid reference if possible).
- Time and nature of accident.
- Extent of injuries.
- Remain by the phone until met by a police officer or member of the rescue team.

Rescue Helicopters
- Secure all loose equipment before arrival of helicopter (weight rucksacks, jackets, etc. with stones).
- Identify yourself by raising your arms in a V as helicopter approaches (do not wave).
- Allow winchman to land of his own accord.
- Do not approach helicopter unless directed to do so by one of the crew (danger from rotors, exhaust, etc.)